Being a Christian Today

Ladislaus Boros

Being a Christian Today

Translated by M. Benedict Davies

A Crossroad Book
THE SEABURY PRESS/NEW YORK

1979
The Seabury Press
815 Second Avenue
New York, N.Y. 10017

Originally published under the title *Heute Christ sein*
© Verlag Herder Freiburg im Breisgau 1978

English translation © Geoffrey Chapman, a division of
Cassell Ltd, 1979

Printed in the United States of America

Library of Congress Cataloging in Publication Data
Boros, Ladislaus, 1927-
Being a Christian today.

Translation of Heute Christ sein.
"A Crossroad book."
1. Christian life—Catholic authors. I. Title.
BX2350.5.B6713   248′.48′2   79-13607
ISBN 0-8164-0440-2

Contents

Preface

This book is concerned with basic Christian attitudes. They belong to the oldest traditions of Christianity—and also to the most revolutionary. Here is a fresh interpretation of them for our times.

A radical change of mind and heart has been taking place ever since the earliest beginnings of Christianity. The radical nature of what I hope to describe is such that it has never fully been put into practice by anyone, not even by the saints. But I state it here in its entirety, for contemporary man, to prevent the same revolution being proclaimed in the world by others who might be intent on using it only for evil purposes.

The truths of Christianity here stated are age-old. In the first part (Basic Principles) I shall try to outline a new type of apologetics. Nowadays the very word arouses our suspicion. Many people fail to understand why a Christian should *defend* his faith. But perhaps it is worth our while considering how a contemporary Christian—in spite of his sense of security and in spite of his doubts—can honestly *show* his faith to the world. In the second section (In Practice) a fresh interpretation of the corporal works of mercy will be attempted. In the third part (Future Prospects) I should like to call the attention of modern man to those very demanding virtues of Christian life known as the spiritual works of mercy. In a fourth section (The Complete Christian) I venture onto a subject which may be of little concern to some of us, but which others will clearly understand. I shall describe the essence of Christian life as set before us by Christ himself in the eight Beatitudes.

I would not wish my reflections to hurt anyone. I intend simply to portray the mind and heart of Christ. This book will be a kind of examination of conscience for some, while those opposed to traditional Christianity may say: 'This is what I have always looked for'. I hope the book will be helpful in either case and that it will be a source of joy.

LADISLAUS BOROS

Translator's Note

Quotations of the Beatitudes are from the Jerusalem Bible, © 1966, 1967, 1968 by Darton, Longman and Todd, Ltd. and Doubleday and Co. Inc., and are used by permission of the publishers. All other Scripture quotations are from the New English Bible, second edition © 1970, by permission of the Oxford and Cambridge University Presses.

The word '*Du*' (familiar form of 'You') has been translated by 'beloved'; when used of God it has been printed with a capital B. The expression 'die *Gesinnung* Christi', a key phrase in the book, has everywhere been translated as 'the *mind and heart* of Christ' since no one English word seemed to convey the richness of meaning of the German word.

Being a Christian Today

1   Basic Principles

In this first section I want to ask tentatively: How can we—Christians of the twentieth century—live out our faith *honestly*? This gives rise to further questions: What is meant by Christian openness? What does it mean for us to have to acknowledge our own failings? What do we mean in our contemporary world by objectivity, by tolerance, by mental unrest?

In the modern world the Christian has become, to a great extent, a loner. He needs to find new forms of friendly meetings with non-Christians. He must have the humility to cease glorying in principles and be prepared to enter into the turmoil of practicalities—duties imposed on him by our times.

This again leads to fresh questions: Are the Christians of our times really honest? In Christianity today is there not a tendency to let disregard for the truth, intellectual mediocrity, self-righteousness and lack of respect for persons hold sway? The contemporary Christian is called to be understanding, to defend human freedom and, above all, to correct his own idea of God.

If this is to be done with integrity further concrete problems arise. For example, how do we intend to build into Christian thinking the theory of evolution? What is the significance of the name 'God' so often thoughtlessly pronounced? Who for us is that mysterious person we call Jesus of Nazareth? What future lies ahead for man? Our God has revealed himself as a God of hope. In this context the contemporary Christian needs to acquire that attitude of hope which his God has shown, revealed in the mind and heart of Jesus Christ. Only in this way will he contribute to the coming of God's kingdom. This means that we must make Christian joy a reality and show genuine love for the world of our times. We conclude with a crucial question: Has Christianity a future? My answer would be 'yes'—on condition that we Christians give offence to no one, make no one our enemy and have the courage to stand as peacemakers between the two 'front lines'.

How can a Christian show his faith?

In our days it is not so easy to defend the Christian faith against other faiths. The word 'apologetics'—defence of the faith—makes people ill at ease. Yet a Christian must see clearly how, even today, he can defend his faith against the world. How can I show the modern world the value and meaning of my faith? We intend to deal with these questions now, beginning with a basic consideration. Our question might be worded: How should the Christian live out his faith today? Ten points, serving as key-words, give a possible answer.

Openness

The Christian has nothing to hide. His faith, insofar as it really is faith, will stand every test. It is precisely when it is contested that it is seen as faith. The 'others', those who think themselves bound to attack our faith, should be taught point by point our reasons for belief. The more honest we are, the more the arguments of our supposed opponent enter into the heart of the matter.

Acknowledgement of one's own mistakes

What we have recognised as the essence of our faith cannot be denied. Here no concessions are possible. But the definitions and manner of expressing it must remain wide open. Occasionally things may go so far that the other exclaims (a recent complaint of an eminent opponent who had the impression of running into open doors on all sides): 'We can have no discussion with you nowadays! You give in on all points!' If we looked at the faith with the eyes of an outsider, seeing the pitiful sort of witness that Christians give, should we ourselves not be tempted to disclaim our faith, and to do so with a clear conscience? The straightforward thing to say is: 'If I expected no more of Christianity than you do, then I should contest it just as you are doing.'

Being human

From the viewpoint of our faith we are convinced that every form of truth is Christian and that therefore everyone seeking truth is in some way one of us.

3

Wherever there is truth, the Church, even in veiled form, is therefore present. This being so, Christian faith is primarily the defence of all that is genuinely human. In the long run it is impossible to contest this effectively. Catholicity means literally universality. It is all-embracing and is taken to include acceptance of truths that turn out to be only partial.

Objectivity

Faith is directed, in the first place, not to feelings but to objects. The objective reality as such is always in some way an image of God and therefore sacred and deserving of respect. And since objectivity is also one of the most hopeful qualities of modern man, this may be Christianity's greatest opportunity today.

Tolerance

For the Christian a human being is always deserving of respect. Tolerance cannot therefore mean for us mere tactics. It is the characteristic attitude of a faith which knows that God himself shows the greatest reverence for the dignity of the person. Christian faith should, then, be tolerant towards intolerance.

The future

Christianity is faith and hope directed towards the future—and contemporary man lives with an eye to the future. In our times, therefore, the best manifestation of Christian faith is to show by our attitude to life that we can be open, that we are the seed of a new

generation of mankind. Our faith consists fundamentally in setting out towards our last end. In this
sense all non-Christians might be said to be reactionary,
whereas all for whom a meaning in the future has
dawned are already, at least anonymously, Christians.

Flexibility
Having fresh ideas is in no way un-Christian. It is time
we granted our theologians, at least occasionally, the
right to say more than just what is acceptable to 'good'
Christians. Over-timidity is no Christian virtue. The
Second Vatican Council showed that theologians who
had previously been denounced prepared the way for
crucial votes which considerably influenced the
discussions and thus made a substantial contribution to
theological progress.

Courtesy
The Christian should never be rude. He should take his
stand clearly for the truth, yes. This is demanded of
him. But the person who gets irritated has already lost.
If a person is too loud in discussion and strikes too hard,
it is always a sign of weakness, indolence and uncertainty. Mental inertia is the last thing our
Christianity can take. A good mind should not be the
exclusive domain of the opponent.

Dialogue
The necessary condition for any genuine dialogue is to
enter into discussion with those who really do have

something to say. Very rarely are they the ones who do the talking in the first instance. The positions of our 'real opponents' (and indeed the ideas underlying such positions) are often a matter of deduction and inference. Once we can convince the 'creators' of these ideas of our genuineness, then the 'spokesmen', so to say—those who actually give voice to them—will be intellectually disarmed.

Mental unrest

In true dialogue one's partner in conversation has to be made to feel uneasy and then he says: 'This man is honest and he is no fool! I too must be understanding and sincere!' At that moment there is a breakthrough. A frank conversation has become possible. Validity of arguments and convictions can be tested. We need no longer be afraid of one another. The other is uneasy about his unbelief. I am uneasy about my faith. The 'lines' have become flexible.

More lies hidden in this brief sketch than a superficial reading might lead one to suppose. Perhaps it is a preliminary outline, in germ, of modern basic theology. The most urgent question might be: What is the position of a Christian in the world of today? What tasks is he faced with? Only after an analysis of this situation can we venture to move on.

The Christian in the contemporary world

We have made an attempt to outline the attitude which should characterise a Christian of our times. The first question was: What is the structure of the world where a Christian bears witness today? In what world-situation should the contemporary Christian be a follower of his Lord?

The Christian as loner

In this new world the Christian feels increasingly that he is alone and, to a certain extent, on his own—that he is fighting for a lost cause. He feels thrown back on his own life—or, more accurately, on his Lord. In her distress the Church can trust only those individuals who are willing and able to translate Christian truth into reality and bear witness to it. There is no enclosure where, as a Christian and a human being, one can feel secure when put to the test in the world. Either we succeed in presenting to the world a new saint, a new man of the world who, by the power of his faith, transforms the world into a new Christendom, or we fail and must then hope for the hour of the dawning of the next world. In this sense we live at a time presenting the greatest opportunity for the faith since the earliest days of Christianity.

New forms of the apostolate

Let us now briefly consider the qualities a Christian of our times should give proof of, if he is to bear witness to

7

his faith. The new type of Christian is living among us here and now. He has a two-fold function: first, he is a man concerned for his fellow man, sympathetic towards others and responsible for them. At the same time he is battling for Christ. He is thus the Church's answer to the present time. It would be misleading to see the task of the apostolate solely as re-establishment of the old order. We must find fresh forms of the apostolate and of pastoral work. We need an apostolate of friendliness, companionship, joy, leisure and hospitality. A society with plenty of leisure is in danger of being overpowered by organised joys of life; a puritanical spirit will be no remedy. A new kind of saint, deeply concerned for the world, is what is needed.

The saint concerned for the world
This new saint will feel he has a responsibility towards the Church as it exists here and now. Zeal for the kingdom of God leaves him no peace. He is involved in the problems of his next-door neighbour and in this neighbour's salvation. A personal apostolate, that of man to man, is built into this concept. The new saint is one who lives in intimate friendship with the Lord. His is a life of prayer and meditation. He makes a daily examination of conscience on his work for God's kingdom. In keeping with his position and his profession he is at pains to be well-informed theologically. He has to be a person capable of understanding the world, that is, life as it really is, and he is deeply concerned with every sphere of it. He has a

sense of what is important; this means that he is quick to seize the moment of grace, in order to sanctify another bit of his surroundings, a fresh part of the world. He is determined to bear witness at every moment and in every sphere of life. The hour of a new kind of sanctification has struck. This venture can be undertaken only by a new kind of saint, by one who has a charism for the contemporary world.

Christian equanimity
Christ's teaching presents an upheaval, a revolution. Christianity is a continuous revolution, but a quiet, non-violent one. The upheaval caused by the Gospel aims at the conversion of individuals, and only in the second place at a transformation of the social, economic and political order. Revolution on the part of Christians comes from within, not from without, from above, not from below. It is non-violent, without bloodshed. Hitherto we have certainly been too prone to regard Christianity as something conservative and preservative. But in reality the teaching of Christ is capable at any time of suspending the privileges of family, nation, rank, education or property in favour of the commandment of love.

Promising signs
During recent pontificates we have experienced an inner renewal. We should like to recall its characteristics: the Eucharistic movement, the liturgical renewal, reflection concerning the sources of theology,

9

Christocentric spirituality, uncloistered religious orders (secular institutes), the discovery of the worldwide mission of the Church, the formation of spheres of work and methods for the lay apostolate and the formulation of a new lay spirituality.

Commitment in the world

Today we must be prepared to help in emergencies connected with welfare, well-being, consumer needs, leisure and education in our society. We Catholics, especially, need the humility to come out of our blissful preoccupation with principles into the stress and strain of the obligations we have a duty to face. In other words—perhaps more easily understood—we must accustom ourselves to come out of the thin, upper atmosphere of theory down to the murky atmosphere of every-day problems and practicalities. It is high time we came to terms with the present situation of the Church, namely, its minority status. Today each individual Christian finds himself subject to the judgment of a world often suspicious and seldom well-disposed. Only when we have shown ourselves trustworthy by our readiness to help and by our real qualifications will non-Christians be prepared to accept that 'extra' which we can offer or bring to their notice. But the Christian also finds himself subject to the judgment of his fellow-Christians in the same world. With them he shares the lot of being an outsider in a society soon to be no longer Christian, or not yet Christian. In our daily dealings with non-Christians we have to show by our lives the excellence of a Christianity that has been under-estimated. The more others feel that we Christians act unobtrusively and indirectly and are ready to serve, the more we use the ordinary human possibilities of communication, the more sympathetic and human we appear as Christians, the nearer this world and those living in it will come to Christ. The Christian must plunge into the world in order to transform it for Christ. The Church, the people of God, should seem to its contemporaries more deserving of love than of respect.

This is the situation where the Christian must prove himself today. We are therefore immediately faced with the question whether Christians have shown them-selves as honest Christians in their dealings with our world.

Are Christians honest?

Here we want to undertake something which may perhaps appear too negative: to point out the failings which hinder us from living out our faith at the present time. There is a hidden ray of hope even in such an insight.

Disregard for the truth
Failure to be intellectually honest is shown by a professional incompetence typical of certain Christian

circles. In our anxiety to justify our viewpoint we are too slow to ask ourselves whether what we want to justify is really true. Even today there is a form of apologetics consisting in an endless chain of half-truths. This deviousness, this effort to appear clever in face of problems, is suspect if a man of integrity feels embarrassment when confronted with them. Why does it often take centuries for us to acknowledge our slightest errors? Pope Leo XIII said: 'God does not need our lies.' Catholicism has no duty to seek alibis for the mistakes of Catholics. The best apologetics certainly do not consist in justifying ourselves by every possible means even when we are clearly in the wrong. Truth is its own advertisement. Today truth is so rare that we are at its mercy when we come across an isolated instance of it.

Intellectual mediocrity

Do we not often get the impression that mental inertia, lack of understanding of one's partner in dialogue, lack of personal qualities and mediocre training are for many Catholics signs of orthodoxy? The kind of orthodoxy we think we can safeguard by mediocrity and mental inertia is the most unsatisfactory in the world. Our ideas are quickly exhausted. Our words fall short even more quickly. As one's intellectual powers are developed, they meet with new factors which throw up fresh, partially unresolved problems. New thresholds must constantly be crossed. There is no going backwards nor even standing still. In intellectual spheres fidelity must always be creative. 'You have rejected knowledge and I will reject you' (Hos. 4, 6). Today, too, God's word is relevant.

The dead corner of history

On this point Karl Rahner has spoken significantly. We have no need to add to what he says:

> Christianity has received no guarantee from God that it cannot sleep away the present time. It may be old-fashioned, it may forget that old truths and values of yesterday are defensible only if, and insofar as, they ensure a new future. And Christianity has to a large extent fallen a prey to this fault, so that today it gives the impression that it is running, with sulks and irritating criticism, behind the wagon in which mankind is journeying towards a new future. The impression emerges that God's eternal revolution in history, where he allows the world to burn in its own eternal fire, is carried out by people who trust only what is old and tried. Such things are basically part and parcel of the world and therefore fragile, ambiguous and temporal; the future and what is still to come is similarly part and parcel of the same world. The duty of the Christian lies in his concrete existence, the historical hour in which he is placed. He may want to be able to handle this hour in a way different from that of the non-Christian. But he has to cope with this hour and no other. Always and everywhere, whenever he escapes into a world of the past, a dream-world, a dead corner of history, a social level which once made the past alive and powerful, not only is his earthly duty neglected, but in addition Christianity suffers from what is artificial, counterfeit and fictitious.

Making light of persons

Today Catholics no longer erect a funeral pyre for a Joan of Arc or a Jan Hus. No one doubts that the Church needs to safeguard purity of doctrine and rectify

13

dangerous trends. But does it have to be done with such incredible indifference for the fate and unhappiness of those affected by the steps taken? It may often be necessary to redress and to correct. But why not with a mother's love? Respect for a person often consists chiefly in respect for his sufferings. Do we show sufficient reverence for the mystery of the human being or do we too easily make light of him?

Self-righteousness

Does the Christian have to perform his actions in order to be seen? Does he necessarily have to embitter his contemporaries by saying: 'We thank thee, God, that we are not like other men'? Must we Catholics so morbidly expect recognition? Christianity really must steer clear of triumphalism! The genuine Christian is not very successful—at least not so successful that he has cause for pride. He has already achieved a great deal if he can give his fellow men a fleeting glance of eternity, despite the massive cloudiness of our times. If we agree on all points we need to be very much on our guard. It means that we have around us people for whom our faith is a matter of indifference. Today we need much more witness and far less propaganda. The saints had only to be present. Their life itself was a challenge. They managed very well without titles, honours, distinctions, uniforms and fanfares. They knew how to command respect by their holiness. They shared what they had, lived in wretched hovels, were abandoned and hungry. A Christianity which has withdrawn from

14

the most pressing duties of love for the poor and the abandoned is—in our opinion—mere talk. It would obviously be completely unjust to maintain that Catholics act in this way. But it is equally certain that in the overwhelming majority of social conflicts too many Catholics have taken their stand quite definitely on one side and it has not always been the side of the poor.

It has been necessary to indicate these negative aspects of Catholicism so that its positive strength may be clear in all its vividness. These negative aspects seem to be the remains of an epoch fast disappearing, with which the Church was associated, indeed had to be associated, in order to fulfil her mandate. Today, however, there are already definite basic trends which take a greater hold on our lives and show that Catholicism is in a position to reach out to the human beings of tomorrow.

Signs of promise

In the last section we pointed out that there are still some faulty attitudes within Catholicism that hinder us from living out our faith with sufficient honesty. We should now like to focus attention on certain attitudes which are proof that new strengths indicative of change are actively at work within us. What are these signs of promise?

Necessity for a sympathetic attitude

The ideological and social crises that have shaken our continent for the past century and a half have also deeply marked Catholic scholars. The theologian has increasingly been obliged to become once more a person who is searching. He has had to struggle with fresh problems and to take note of new thinking in matters concerning revelation. He has found courage to launch out into new domains of theology, to discuss, to reconsider the 'tools' used for theological concepts. This change in the Christian approach—for it is not in any way confined to theology—did not arise from a desire for novelty. We were obliged by others to look for new answers to new questions. In all this a mental attitude inherent in Christianity was obvious. It has always refused to be a religion for the initiated. An approach has continually been left open for all. Only rarely has anyone noticed the Church as a real pioneer of universal democracy. She attacked intellectual slavery at its roots. Even in the Middle Ages the Church opposed teaching 'two-fold truth' with all her might. She thus revealed her basic attitude towards truth: every truth comes from God and is therefore deserving of deep reverence. We are open to all truth, independently of the person proclaiming it. This attitude means that Christianity can never become antiquated. It is not a closed religion, it is wholly open.

Call to freedom

Freedom is not so much man's claim on God as God's

claim on man. To be free is a divine obligation. Christianity is moreover the religion of the most radical freedom because it is a religion of deification. A divine being cannot be manufactured. Not even God can do this. It can take place only in a life with God, a life freely chosen. Never was human freedom treated with such fundamental respect as by Jesus Christ. Neither can people be 'steamrollered' into the faith by having it shouted in their ears. The Church—in theory if not always in practice—has continually remained faithful to the principle of radical freedom. In her teaching on freedom she presents the conscience of an individual as the ultimate authority for salvation. Even when the conscience is erroneous, it must be followed. One does not become a Christian by fleeing from subjective uncertainty into the sphere of objective certainty. At the deepest level in our lives we are never certain. When Joan of Arc was asked if she was in a state of grace, instinctively she gave *the* answer of a Christian: 'If I am, may the Lord preserve me in it. If I am not, may God place me in it.' But because Christianity affirms freedom, even to the extent of the most radical uncertainty, it is shown as the religion of the whole human race, inclusive of a new and different human race.

Correcting our image of God

One of the most hopeful signs of contemporary Christianity is that people no longer speak with such confidence about God. They do not pretend to know all his mysteries. God's transcendence has become

17

paramount for us today. This—in our opinion—is one of the graces of our times. Instinctively, a contemporary Christian rejects the numerous caricatures of God: the image of the 'policeman' apparently concerned only with infringements of the law; the image of the universal 'accountant' following up with frightening accuracy the list of our actions; the image of the useful 'stop-gap' dealing with the logic of the world; the image of the mighty 'magician' perpetually allowing himself to be called upon to explain cosmic phenomena (the process of evolution, the origin of life and its various spheres); the image of the dreadful 'torturer' apparently intent only on chasing into hell the unfortunate coloured peoples and children who die unbaptised. If today we have cause to be grateful to atheists it is because, by their continual objections, they prevent us from cheating in our dealings with God. The processes in contemporary Christianity show with what extraordinary versatility Christian thought confronts profane knowledge and why there is no reason to fear any change in man and his view of life.

Humbleness of mind
A critical mind, ever measuring itself against the truth, and therefore ultimately a humble mind, is one of the best qualities of modern man. It corresponds moreover to the Christian attitude of mind and has nothing to do with agnosticism properly so called. It is basically an enthusiastic love for reality. Henri Bergson remarked very appositely that realism is one of the outstanding

18

qualities of the true mystic. The best Christian is not the one who most easily allows himself to be taken in. It is not often actually put into words that within faith itself lies an agnosticism that is completely justified, an agnosticism whose real name is mystery. A Christian who thinks he has fathomed all God's plans has either lost his appreciation of God or he is a cheat. Contemporary theology is very conscious that the manner of expressing mysteries continually lags behind their uncreated content. In our modern understanding of a mystery emphasis is laid on the fact that the incomprehensibility of the mystery is not removed even in the vision of God, but that the vision of the incomprehensible–eternal in its incomprehensibility is actually what constitutes eternal bliss. We can never catch up with God. Therefore it is possible for us, eternally and without interruption, to grow into Him. So today's theologian must continually search for fresh formulation of mysteries. It is good that these thoughts have become commonplace in today's Christianity.

We have set out in this section signs of promise. What is to be said of Christianity when the negative and positive signs are compared? Have we a future ahead of us?

A preliminary balance-sheet

Let us now pause in our deliberations and reflect on what we have done so far. In the first section we tried to describe the basic attitude required of a Christian if he is to show his faith to others. Then we outlined the qualities of the world where a Christian of today must prove his faith. Next we enumerated the characteristics which show that Christian.lives are, to a certain extent, lacking in honesty. Finally we noted the positive traits which, in contemporary Christianity, point towards the future. We did not pass over anything in silence. Obviously, we could sketch only broad outlines for reflection. Very few examples were given. But this was not our task, since the reader can easily, from examples in his own experience, complete the outlines. Now we should like to draw up a preliminary balance-sheet, in order to establish fundamental principles from which a genuinely Christian method of giving witness can be worked out.

Challenge

First of all, as a result of our previous questions, we would point out that nowhere in his present situation can the Christian meet the contemporary world as if he were an undisturbed proprietor. In our times everything is in motion in one way or another. Criticism against the Church often arises from the fact that people are fascinated by the challenges of Christianity but, at the same time, they observe how little the lives of Christians correspond to them. Being a Christian faced with this type of challenge means that a man's religion—for example, love of one's enemy—is not inherited as a legacy like some piece of family furniture. Nor is it found in the cradle or behind the pillars of a cathedral. No, not even in the baptismal font. It can be gained only by the surrender of the whole person. The essence of being a Christian consists in the total gift of a finite person to God, and in this gift the person receives the total gift of God. Thus Christianity has already outstripped all world ideologies of the future. We need witnesses to show that this outstripping has already begun. This is the most powerful challenge of Christianity to Christians and the first fundamental principle of all witness to the faith.

Witness

Some years ago Hans Urs von Balthasar pointed out that what is Christian always carries with it a reference to martyrdom. This does not necessarily have to be death—it may be just frustration or being called to failure. But at the heart of his convictions is something for which the Christian is prepared to die: here is found eternity in its temporal nature and concept. No Christian is called upon to reflect on all the mysteries and to witness to everything with equal insistence. He has the right, even the duty, to enter more deeply into mystery in those areas to which he feels a special calling, in keeping with his total self-surrender. This will be his individual life, in grace, with his special charism. Another important point is that the Christian should give his witness in the attitude of a martyr, that is, with a complete lack of self-defence. It really is a case of not defending oneself. A personal testimony such as this might be the second element of Christian witness today. There is a third element connected with it.

Integrity

The expression 'integrity' means that a man's character, speech and actions are such that, at all times, and to all men, they can be justified. To Christian integrity belongs too the courage for mental decision, even when the decision is subject to all the uncertainty, darkness and danger inherent in decisions of a finite mind limited by space and time. This leads us to reflect that Christian testimony itself must have its place in history. Similarly, faith itself has to take time. A genuine attitude of faith has often to let questions ride. There are many questions concerning faith where an honest Christian is entitled to recognise his incompetence—with modesty, but at the same time with courage. What should every Christian profess unconditionally? It is hard to say. Christendom is no fortress of truth with countless rooms where one must dwell in order to remain in the truth. Christianity is much more an opening within the world which, from individual truths, leads to *the* truth, to the incomprehensibility of God. To concede all this might be the third essential element of Christian witness.

Joy of living

The basic attitude of Christians which permeates all other attitudes is that of joy. Joy is the predominant spirit of Christian life, the spirit of the Good News (the Gospel). For the Christians of the early Church Christ 'came to bring life', he was the 'first-born from the dead', the 'beginning of the new creation', 'first fruits', the 'beginning of the new world'. Today these New Testament titles of honour given to Christ have to some extent fallen into oblivion and our redeemer is seen as 'prince of life', as 'guide of the whole of creation', as 'spearhead' of the universal becoming. This cosmic position of Christ gives rise in Christian life to universal goodwill. Since Christ's resurrection life can no longer be a failure. Life was finally established in the risen body of the redeemer. It has become infinitely precious and safeguards our passage to eternal fulfilment. Into this basic attitude of an all-pervading joy—which constitutes the fourth element of Christian witness—all other expressions of Christian life should be integrated.

Selflessness

The radiating transparency of Christian life—that is, all that we have hitherto mentioned—is the foundation of Christian selflessness. This selflessness is the measure and norm of Christian fulfilment of life: self-conquest, delicacy in encounters with others and sensitivity for one's neighbour. This attitude becomes a reality only in those for whom the other person, instead of oneself, is the centre of life. A Christian who takes himself in hand can give himself entirely to others. He does this with no idea of gain and so he becomes completely open. He no longer has his eyes fixed on himself but is devoted to the service of his neighbour, his brother, his sister. Selflessness is an indication of a deep and very sincere way of life. That readiness to receive, expressed by Christ in the unforgettable words 'poor in spirit', is put into practice and this alone makes it possible at the end of life to reach out to God empty-handed and to receive from Him, as an unmerited gift, complete fulfilment. In this sense of selflessness is the fifth element of Christian witness in the contemporary world.

We have tried to outline the basic attitude which should characterise the Christian of our day as he meets his fellow men. Such an attitude would indeed be genuine and convincing. The foundations are now laid for further reflection. The next step is to ask what questions concerning faith should be answered with special emphasis for contemporary man. What kind of faith is handed on in dialogue?

Faith handed on in dialogue

Christian dialogue with the world has begun. By world I mean a diversity defined as pluralistic and scientific, but also a Christian society with widely differing views (sometimes even with rifts). It is a world where the Christian has to enter into open dialogue. It is also a world which is to characterise the Church of tomorrow.

In all our efforts to hand on the faith we need to be aware of this situation because it provides the challenge to answer essential questions for our fellow men. The following are the kind of questions we are asked today.

The question of the theory of evolution
Christian theology must see clearly that because of evolutionary thought (on which, to a great extent, the meaning of the world is now based) certain theological concepts, hitherto seen as firmly established, are threatened, if not shattered. If the theory of evolution is correct, the Christian is obliged to answer this type of question: In what sense is it true that God created man? If one sees the development of the world—as evolution does—as a single unbroken, continuous whole, what is meant by the turning-points in the history of the universe which we are accustomed to call paradise, the fall, redemption, the cross, resurrection, the powers of evil and the transformation of the world at the end of time? What justification have we for saying that Christ—as the perfect fulfilment of man and of the universe—necessarily became man? Above all, can one in a single overall vision embrace nature and super-nature, world and grace, what is humanly attainable and what is God-given? Can one see in Christ the 'glorified point of convergence' of mankind and of all being? It is certainly worthwhile attempting to answer all these questions on the basis that everything evolves. Even if our answers are not satisfactory, we shall discover that revelation contains elements other than those

hitherto treated in our dogmatic theology. Anyone who could give these problems an answer rooted in theology, logically well thought out, biblically valid, would indeed be a theologian for the future.

The question of God

In the contemporary world this question would include answers to the problems of atheism and unbelief. It is something more than a mere 'enquiry into God'; it is also an enquiry into how far it is possible for the man of our times to entertain a genuine experience of God. Here we must be aware of the fact that for modern man God is not really relevant in our world. We must therefore consider seriously this experience of the *absence* of God and try to interpret it in a new way. Finally, we should have to ask ourselves in all honesty where, why and how people today have this experience of God being absent. Perhaps we should often leave God a free hand, sincerely recognising the limitations of a finite existence.

The question of Christ

This question must be answered for the contemporary world from the standpoint of salvation history and world history, showing that these include within their purview the whole of humanity from its inception, and that the true consummation of the whole of history is to be found in Christ. Here we should perhaps develop to the full that transition between the historical Jesus and the Christ of faith already present in the earliest christology. The essence of Christianity is Jesus Christ the person, a Christ who identified himself radically with his fellow man as his brother or sister. In this connection we might bring home to contemporary man an unexpected point, by showing him how his characteristic attitude (concern for his fellow man) really constitutes a concern for Christ. In this view the whole sphere of human relationships is seen as comprising one single reality: it includes friendship and love, faithfully lived out—in other words the real and genuine practice of human fellowship and the building up of the Body of Christ—the making real, that is to say, of that which transposes the world and mankind into the dimension of eternal life.

The question of man

The form in which Christian teaching is presented should be such that in it contemporary man can recognise his own *de facto* experience of himself. This teaching therefore includes the primeval unity of nature and grace, and it does not remove what we call grace to the realms beyond concrete human experience. It is teaching concerning man which does not simply relegate love, the experience of death, experiences of despair and meaninglessness to pious literature. We should make clear to our contemporaries that it is not so important to have a clearly articulated concept of God as to feel oneself called upon to recognise one's neighbour as a brother, to offer him a helping hand, to show him our sympathy and tolerance, to overcome

27

one's own self-centred attitude and dispositions. God would not have become man if we had been able to find him in another way, outside human life and somewhere else, other than in our neighbour.

The question of the 'last things'

In their view of salvation history Christians must think out much more radically the connection between the individual and collective future. Nor can we any longer take it for granted nowadays that modern man entertains hope of eternal life: an attitude to which he must be gently introduced. A theology of hope is something that still has to be developed out of the dry formulae of our scholastic theology. In his book *Das Prinzip Hoffnung* Ernst Bloch strives to give full weight to the radical (i.e. from the roots upwards) significance of hope as a human attitude, to recognise it as a force that transforms human living and shapes history, and finally to enquire into its ultimate orientation. The fact that nowadays this is something that a Marxist has to do should put Christian thinkers to shame. For it is precisely we Christians who bear upon our flesh the brand of 'hope as a principle of life' as no one else does. The reason for the surprisingly widespread response to Ernst Bloch's philosophy of hope is surely that it places our puny wishes and dreams in a universal perspective and thus recognises hope as the real driving force of the world. This gives the Christian thinker sufficient material on which to examine his conscience. Has it not become fashionable among ourselves to make much of the wretched condition of mankind? Many a writer has won himself a smattering of literary fame in this way. Ernst Bloch has taught us how hope and a taste for happiness constitute an authentic element in human (and *a fortiori* Christian) living.

Even these sketchy indications already provide an outline for handing on the faith in dialogue. One of the most pressing duties today is to work this out in detail. In so doing we should have to undertake a thorough re-thinking of Christian doctrine. This is the need, the opportunity and the grace for Christian teaching in the contemporary world.

God of the future

The basic thoughts of this section have been expressed by the apostle Paul in his second letter to the Corin-thians: 'The Son of God, Jesus Christ, is the "yes" pronounced upon God's promises. It is through Him that we say "Amen"' (2 Cor. 1, 20). What are God's promises? Where have they been revealed? What form have they assumed in human consciousness? If we look into these questions it becomes clear that Jesus Christ and his resurrection do not represent an event in isolation from the 'becoming' of the world and mankind. What these events signify, rather, is that grace has transcended law—law, that is, considered as a state to which all spheres of worldly existence have been subject from their very origins.

The development of the world

God's promises, of which the risen Christ is the fulfilment, can already be deduced from the 'event of creation'. On the level of experience, this event is seen as a process of becoming or evolution. We can better express the development of the world in terms of the basic law of 'becoming new', as something that is dominated by the law of 'self-improvement'. Cosmic development 'works its way upwards' from an original state of being. It evolves Milky Ways, solar systems and planets. Right from its most basic beginnings it presses forwards towards ever more complex material systems. It searches for the 'upward path', and thus creates at first primitive and then ever more complex forms of life. The quest takes many paths, and, in its details, may appear almost devoid of direction. Yet despite this, the development of the world, viewed as a whole, traces an ascending line. The universe 'gropes its way' toward awareness. Hence cosmic development is not a static phenomenon but a single unified process of becoming. What emerges at its culmination is a being who constitutes the apex of evolutionary creation, the outcome of a process of cosmic striving which has lasted for millions upon millions of years. This being is man. In this development of the cosmos we can discern one significant factor: in its growth the world improves upon itself, excels itself, raises itself up. Throughout the cosmos phenomena gradually emerge which cannot be deduced from what preceded them. This in itself reveals the basic structure of the emerging world: the production of something which cannot be explained in terms of what went before.

How humanity improves upon itself

Man himself, viewed in his place in the cosmic system, does not consider himself as a finished product. Initially he constitutes only a preliminary draft of his true self. He has been commissioned to create himself and to realise the fulness of his own nature. All that the process of cosmic development has produced is that basic material of existence from which man must shape himself by his own efforts and so bring himself to the 'apex of cosmic being'. The forward thrust of cosmic development assumes in man, it is true, a new form. But the direction of this thrust remains the same: improvement upon the existing self. The cosmic energy accumulating within us comes to life in our awareness in the forms of dreams, hopes, longings and restlessness. Thus concentrated within us, the whole scope of the evolutionary process generates in human awareness a powerful impetus of ideas, desires and presentiments. No one individual can prevent his life from being open to the infinite. No individual can escape the secret desire to break out of the straitened circumstances of his own life. Man is preoccupied with what is expected of him—and such great expectations are immeasurable. Because they are immeasurable, all

31

his experiences are open to that which is ineffable and incalculable. The expectation of something greater, something unattainable by our own powers, and precisely for that reason totally fulfilling, is a basic characteristic of human living. The true birth of man is something that is constantly in process of becoming. But is the situation such that man can bring it to completion by his own resources? Unfortunately—or rather fortunately—no. Here we have reached the nub of the matter. The true nature of man is unattainable by man's own powers. Human existence infinitely transcends the self.

Let us insert here a brief interim consideration and bring the first two points together. We have recognised, as an element intrinsic to the material cosmos, a dynamic bias towards cognitive forms of life. By producing man it transcends itself. Man himself, in the achievement of his own life, carries further this same dynamic impulse intrinsic to the development of the cosmos and of humanity. Now if this process is to have any sense at all, then at some point the development involved must lead to a human being capable of achieving definitively and totally the breakthrough to that which is wholly other. On this showing the birth of the Son of God—as we have already indicated—in no sense constitutes a 'disruptive intervention' into the world on the part of the Absolute. In the God-Man all that our world has been dreaming of right from the beginning has found its fulfilment. The incarnation—

and in fact the resurrection—of the God-man constitutes fundamentally the grace-given fulfilment of a tendency that is basic to the created order. Right from the very origins of the world the 'principle of resurrection' has been at work. The entire created order and the history of humanity constitute one single sphere of resurrection.

The resurrection of Christ

In his earthly life Jesus Christ had already overcome the misery of human existence. For him, therefore, even death did not constitute a complete break. In the death of Jesus a factor which had already been operating in the temporal conditions of his earthly life achieved its definitive form: it was the total fulfilment of human living. On careful scrutiny of the Gospel accounts of the resurrection we can discern a profound transformation in the disciples' own understanding of Christ. What they perceived was this: the final state of existence as emerging from the fulfilment of what is earthly. In the resurrection of Christ human existence attains a dimension which transcends the loftiest peaks of creaturehood in its process of becoming. It has entered into the life of the Blessed Trinity. Thus what has been achieved in the risen Christ is the salvation history of the cosmos: God has descended into the depths of the world and assumed our nature so that with it he can rise above everything that the world is capable of producing. By reproducing the earthly mode of Christ we too become sharers in the infinitude of being of the

Absolute, and at the same time we bring to its fulness the process of becoming of the cosmos.

This insight is fully exploited in the New Testament understanding of faith, especially in the Pauline writings: Christ has come to us indeed—yet for all this he continues to be, right to the end of time, continually in the act of 'coming'. Throughout the whole of world history Christ is 'growing' in us. Christians build up the risen Body of Christ. Not until the end of time will the *pleroma tou Christou*, the 'full Christ', be present. This means that Christians stand at the highest point of development of the cosmos. When the 'measure of Christ' is fulfilled, when all men who are intended to constitute the fulness of being of Christ have surrendered their lives to Christ, creation is complete. Then new life begins: Christ will yield up to the embrace of the Father that reality of his which has grown up within the dimension of humanity and of the universe. The adventure of the world will be drawn to its conclusion. The cosmos will be transformed and will achieve its final and definitive mode of being. The life of happiness without end can begin.

This means that the aspect which humanity will bear will be for all eternity the countenance of God. But how can we—men of today—encounter Jesus Christ? How can we bring the mind and heart of Christ to its fulness in our own lives? This is the fundamental question of Christian living.

The mind and heart of Christ

How can a contemporary Christian encounter the 'God of the future'? Our answer was given in the last section: insofar as he makes the mind and heart of Christ effective in his life. But what do we mean by 'the mind and heart of Christ'? To answer questions like this, Christian theology has to become once more unbiassed in its teaching. This is especially necessary where we are concerned with bringing back into the light of experience truths now buried, but taken for granted by Christians and seen as indispensable. First we must describe the mind and heart of Christ (and the consequent demands made upon us) and then ask more precisely what exactly was the heart of the teaching of Jesus Christ.

The essential beginning of a life of faith is the effort to accept the mind and heart of Christ interiorly and to radiate it in the world. This happens by the transformation of one's whole life, by making one's own that inspiration for thought and action which animated Christ's life. All other efforts, thoughts, words and teaching are, in the last analysis, secondary. The beginning of 'being a Christian' takes place in that realm of life to which Christ addressed himself in his very first preaching: 'Repent; for the kingdom of God is upon you' (Matt. 4, 17). The key concept of Christian living is therefore *change of mind and heart.*

A change of mind and heart grows out of a relationship with Christ. From being lost in externals a person learns to concentrate on the one essential which is at the heart of all he does and thinks. This complete transformation is a return to the essence of human living, a return to one's origin. Quietly and unassumingly, thoughtfully, ready to make decisions, a Christian should examine the whole spectrum of his life with reference to its fundamental basis. In this process a Christian mind and heart will be formed in him. These dispositions will show the meaning of a person's life, his singleness of heart with reference to good and evil and to true and false. The Christian commits himself to this venture of complete transformation of his life by trying to make the mind and heart of Christ his own. How was the mind and heart of Christ expressed? Christ was a *God for persons*.

He was the Word coming from the Spirit of love. In his heart he bore human affliction and transformed it into a light burning within him. He was harsh towards the self-righteous and stern where the under-privileged were threatened by the arrogant. But he was always at hand when people were distressed or in despair. He spent himself generously and unobtrusively that all might receive his joy and peace. We can only attempt very cautiously to couch in frail human words the mystery of the mind and heart of Christ—the real heart of our faith. Christ's friends witnessed the fate of someone whose greatness consisted first and foremost in the fact that he entered into all the narrowness of our human life and always, though often tired out, managed to find a kind word for his friends. The *goodness and human kindness of God appeared in Christ.*

To the disconsolate he showed the way to joy. With the weary he shared a new zest for life, a simple cheerfulness and the possibility of a saving change of heart. Courage for such transformation came from Christ himself. Every gesture and every word were tokens of his simplicity, his modesty and his readiness to help. He never sought self-glorification but took upon himself that sense of worthlessness which all real love experiences .at times. He saw before him people who—like the tax-collector—were far from God and did not dare to raise their eyes to heaven. His look penetrated deep into the heart of man and into eyes full of tears and lost hopes. When he could see no other way of helping he knelt down—as in the washing of the disciples' feet—ready to give all he had. We can therefore conclude that the central message of the Christian faith is . . .

The news of Christ's resurrection
This man who was so generous and understanding was put to death. There were some for whom the delicacy of his kindness was more than they could bear. The friends of Christ recognised, by their faith after the resurrection, that the mind and heart of Christ had a validity that was absolute, whatever the world's opinion on the subject. One of the essential characteristics of the experience of the resurrection was that goodness, human kindness, forgiveness and affection are the ultimate

37

norm of life. In his attitude during his earthly life Jesus of Nazareth showed us the essence of true manhood. Since then everyone who in all honesty is truly human translates into reality the mind and heart of Christ.

No power in the world can any longer deprive us of Christ. In his resurrection Christ has said his eternal 'yes' to all that is intended to be sincere, to all gentleness and forgiveness, to all goodness and hope. Jesus Christ, God become man, become human, demands of us above all human kindness sincerely lived out—with all that goes with such kindness: sympathy for what is strange to us, reverence for the qualities of other human beings, patience in our difficulties, endurance, respect, fidelity, gratitude, selflessness and above all courtesy. He asks of us respect for every creature and an unselfish goodwill towards creation. He begs us to meet others with respect, to defend the lowly and defenceless, to suffer in silence, to judge no one and thus to meet God in man. Our God is a human God. He demands of us, as an essential living out of our faith, first and foremost, simple human kindness. This would seem to be the basic factor of our Christian life, learnt from the mind and heart of Christ.

The consequence of all this for us is that Christianity is not really doctrinal teaching or a rule of life. It is that too, but that is not the heart of it. The essence of Christianity is not a doctrine, but a person, Jesus of Nazareth, his concrete life, work and fate. For

Christians a person, not a doctrinal statement, is the supreme rule of life.

But to avoid misunderstandings we must add that Christ never taught a vague humanism. His claims cut deep into human life. The 'kingdom of God' which formed the content of his life's work was at the centre of all he did. Christ's thoughts, actions and fate were concentrated on the kingdom. In his teaching Christ meant by 'kingdom of God' that God reigns in us.

The kingdom of God

When we speak of the mind and heart of Christ we must not lose sight of what was the centre of Christ's teaching: the kingdom of God. Jesus Christ came to us to reveal God who is sovereign over our world. He came to tell us what God thinks of us, how we stand before him and what he expects *of* us. He came to tell us what God wants to do *for* us. Fundamentally, becoming a Christian means accepting, on the words of Jesus, God's action as ultimate principle and norm of our life. The centre of Christ's teaching was the kingdom of God. Two texts from Christ's revelation are especially significant for us: 'The time has come; the kingdom of God is upon you' (Mark 1, 14) and 'You cannot tell by observation when the kingdom of God comes. There will be no saying, "Look, here it is!" or "There it is", for in fact the kingdom of God is among you' (Luke 17, 20–21). The life-style of Christians in the world arose

39

from the tension here clearly indicated between 'upon you' and 'not yet revealed'. Christ chose for himself humility and self-surrender. This choice led to the establishment of a kingdom within. Christ willed to set up an inner activity secretly at work in the world. He willed to create in us an inner principle of life from which would flow in a hidden way powers that would form and transform us. He was not concerned with finding solutions to problems which man should answer for himself. We might try to clarify this teaching of Jesus about the kingdom of God by considering a view that perhaps has not been put into words before.

A Christian must not entertain hatred

Christ demanded of those who wished to be with him hatred towards no one, no returning of evil for evil. He even demanded of them love for their enemies. Christ's life was simple and unobtrusive. His love of powerlessness was not weakness; he assumed this attitude that he might remain very close to everyone. Here we see the first basic quality of the kingdom proclaimed by Christ: a kingdom having an element of hatred is not the kingdom of God.

Unobtrusiveness

Christ enjoyed the small everyday things of life: a good meal, a refreshing drink, a pleasant walk, a real friendship. He always met people unobtrusively in order not to dazzle them. Young at heart, fearless before the mighty ones of this world, he was able to bring about conversion to holiness. The Good News was his whole life. 'I have spoken thus to you that my joy may be in you, and your joy complete' (John 15, 11). The fruits of his Spirit are: 'joy, peace, patience and kindness' (Gal. 5, 22). The Apostles understood this nearness to Christ in human life as a challenge: 'You are transported with a joy too great for your souls' (1 Pet. 1, 8). Christ was at pains to avoid titles. In his life he set a pattern of remarkable loneliness, that loneliness peculiar to the abyss, the mountain-top and the sea. Anyone who aspires to penetrate into the nature of a mystery must spend long hours alone in order to be able to concentrate on what is essential. By contemplation—with no personal gain in view—Jesus sensed the nature and meaning of things. His earth was earthly, with his parables flowing through it almost as its life-blood. His life was characterised by peace and detachment. His speech, matter-of-fact and at the same time open to the Absolute, is proof of this; his conversation takes much for granted and wastes no words. A kingdom that is spectacular and parades famous names is not the kingdom of God.

Receptiveness

Christ's life was dominated by silence. His was a listening heart. He kept things to himself and did not push himself forward. Christ did not allow his life to be dominated by habit. He made himself available for people. The fact that Christ's friends called him a 'good man' may not be the most significant statement of

41

Christology. But the man who has learnt—perhaps by bitter experience—the meaning of human kindness knows that only a God-man is able to give proof of this title at all times. On this subject an important question was asked about Jesus: In what form is the Messiah to appear? In his thoughts about God and the super-natural help He gives, a man is apt to look for sensation and excitement. But this was not God's will for Christ; his was simple, humble service of his neighbour in the nitty-gritty of life. Christ did not wish to be seen as a superman but came to his own people as an unknown person from a distant market-town, as a sympathetic member of his suffering nation. The only power he wanted to exercise was that of humility. If a kingdom is not humble and insignificant, it is not the kingdom of God.

Unassumingness
Jesus came from a family and tribe that was poor and he made no attempt to improve its status. His poverty was unassuming. In all that he did and in all that happened to him he was singularly unsuccessful. In Christ's life there is a complete lack of what we call 'being understood'. When we read the Gospel we get the impression of a bitter—but not embittered—inner composure, a silence in spite of the words 'The light shines on in the dark, and the darkness has never mastered it' (John, 1, 5). Christ accepted that his fate was inevitable. When he died, abandoned by God, his rejection reached its utmost limits. Christ willed to live

in the world of the poor. In bearing witness he willed to stake all. The people who waited for him were poor people who really had only one escape, and that was no escape at all: an excess of work and of oppression. Nowhere was there love ready to help them, nowhere any possibility of protection. The 'poor of Yahweh' were people destined by a mysterious divine law to disappear unnoticed from this world with all their cares and sufferings as if they had never existed. Such people waited longingly for Christ and he had no right to ignore those who, in uprightness of heart, had surrendered in this way to God. If a kingdom makes claims and is rich, it is not the kingdom of God.

We conclude that the kingdom of God is characterised by absence of hatred, by insignificance and by lack of pretensions. It is not really easy to say whether the Christian of today gives evidence of these qualities. Probably he does not. He should strive to acquire them. If not, there would be no Christians and the Church would not be the Church of Christ. However, our efforts suffice. Christ does not ask of us all or nothing. Sincere goodwill is enough but this there must be.

Christian joy
When we speak about the Christian of today we cannot omit two important Christian qualities: joy and love. In

contemporary man there is often a deeply-rooted mistrust of joy. Here we want to mention three prerequisites of Christian joy and then indicate a way leading to it.

Service of one's neighbour

Christian joy is not an enthusiasm foreign to our world. As a person becomes selfless and goes out to his fellow men, he experiences joy. Self-giving provides us with courage for the reality which we may describe as real joy. In general, when we try to move out of our absorption with what is petty, we shall notice that there is a hidden energy in us. What leads to the service of our neighbour?

On Ascension Day the disciples went home with great joy after Christ had been removed from their sight. One might say: an unusual kind of joy. Christ had been withdrawn from their sight. Before this the disciples had indeed been overjoyed. A new kind of presence of Christ had been given them as a result of the Easter events. For example, they had felt 'their hearts on fire'. But a still more significant transformation took place on Ascension Day. For the first time it became clear to the disciples that from now on they must no longer 'look up into the sky' but enter upon their duty on earth in order to find joy. They had to learn by experience that Christ had gone away from them and that, if they wished to find joy and fulfilment, they too must go out of themselves.

The Ascension guided the disciples into the world.

They went to Jerusalem, chose Matthias and preached at Pentecost. They experienced harsh altercations with their own people. They began to feel the friction caused by the early Chruch in its slow formation and unseen growth. They became more deeply involved in problems, afflictions, worldly quarrels, and they experienced the miseries and obscure windings and twistings of the world. They were spared nothing. But an invisible joy grew ceaselessly within them. Beyond the afflictions, poverty, humiliations and wrongs, they saw with eyes able to sense the invisible that the Spirit of reconciliation was hovering over them. The Spirit of joy was in the world at last. This divine joy went with the disciples on their journeys through the world: 'In all our many troubles my cup is full of consolation, and overflows with joy' (2 Cor. 7, 4). Here we have discovered a basic law of Christian joy: to enter into the afflictions of our neighbour, take his load upon ourselves and share with him his burden of oppression. This is the Christian way to happiness. But it also means the last place. Our help is given silently, we are peacemakers in the world. In our joy, if we want to be first, we must take the last place.

Self-denial
In giving joy to others one usually experiences joy oneself. This is the conclusion of our reflection so far. Joy can also be the fruit of a conscious effort. So the following statement is valid in the life of a Christian: the path to joy is by way of self-denial. But all Christian

45

self-denial is at the service of fulfilment, all death to self takes place only for the sake of bringing life. To value suffering, renunciation and self-denial as an end would be foolish. There is enough suffering in our world. Selflessness in the service of our neighbour makes possible the apparently impossible. The saints speak— they even rejoice and sing—while enduring terrible interior and exterior afflictions. Francis of Assisi felt he had to seize two pieces of wood and play on them as if with violin and bow, he felt he had to dance and sing. At the same time he was desperately poor and completely powerless. Francis Xavier, for sheer joy, like a child at play, threw an apple into the air and caught it again, while he trod the icy-cold fields in a Japanese winter, stripped of everything and dogged by failure. We experience joy only if we are selfless. This is the secret of Christian joy: selflessness is the condition of finding joy in every situation in life even when, according to human standards, we might be sad. If we are wrapped up in ourselves, we are depressed by whatever attacks us: illness, suffering, poverty, disgrace, failure. If we have become selfless, everything we suffer is unimportant and as nothing. Surely a life like this is proof that there is an Absolute in our world. If nowadays we often find it impossible to pray, as Christians we should at least radiate joy in the world. Possibly this would be our Christian prayer.

In the world but not of the world
At the beginning of the third century Clement of

46

Alexandria spoke of the basic tension of Christian life, i.e. the basic tension of joy, as follows: the perfect Christian is 'in the world but not of the world'. This is a very sound formula for Christian living.

On the one hand the Christian should be convinced that his earthly life is unimportant and that this life is followed by an eternal state of rejoicing. He should not take things too seriously: for him nothing is important enough. A Christian life cannot therefore be shattered; Christian fulfilment lies beyond all that is in the world. On the other hand it is clear that the same Christian must move out of this radical otherworldliness and go into our world. It is by this attitude that he shows serious consideration for the world. Because God is greater than everything, he is to be found everywhere, even in the most unimportant things. He can meet us in every street. Such an attitude gives rise to an unfailing readiness to detect the call of God in all the situations of life and to feel a joy that is without strain. The inscription on the tomb of Ignatius of Loyola—'It is God-like not to be hemmed in by what is great and yet to remain involved in what is small'—might be a motto for joy for contemporary man. The man of our times should know no limits where greatness is concerned. The greatest and most holy is not great enough or holy enough for him. His desires should always go beyond his achievements. And yet he should seek his great God everywhere, even in the smallest things. These would seem to be a few principles and conditions for genuine Christian joy in our times.

47

The demands of love

Love is the basic attitude of the Christian towards reality. First one should provide contemporary man with a clear idea of what real love is. This is only possible if we make use of three very simple, perhaps over simple, ideas: action, sharing and service.

Action: The existence of the loved one must be bearable in the world. This is not brought about by mere words. By unfailing love one must *create* life for the beloved and assure inner growth for him. Love is first and foremost selfless action.

Sharing: Love creates unity of being. From this emerges the state of 'being-with', that is, the unity of two natures as brought about by the exercise of mutual love.

Service: The one who really loves must lose himself. He should learn how a loved one can be enriched by our care, how someone, cared for at the cost of oneself, can grow and flourish.

It is clear that these three ideas of the nature of love say very little. At least we have defined the form of love. The ideas have indicated what we do not intend to speak about. What then is Christian love in our times? It is important to note that this is not fundamentally different from the love of God for us, reproduced in the created sphere. This was always true—today more so than ever. We should like now to attempt to outline God's love for us and to ask ourselves how we can make this love truly human today. How does God love us?

God gives

God's love for us is essentially a giving. We must be clear on one point: God does not only love, his nature *is* love. Everything he does has its ultimate reason in his love. Therefore God's giving is inevitable. Perhaps we should reflect on another point: God *has* nothing because he *is* everything. Accordingly, God can give nothing except himself.

The Christian must try to reproduce in his own life today something of the nature of God's love. This means, in practice, that he must give himself unstintingly. His giving must be independent of the response from the beloved. It also means that he must give himself away, as a free gift. The Christian should so act that there is always something of himself in his gifts. This would be a Christian love divinely lived out: giving without reason and giving oneself.

God's indwelling

Everything created, nature and supernature, lives insofar as it bears within it the traits of the second divine Person. The development of creation happens through God's becoming ever more present in the world. What does this mean in terms of our Christian love? The Christian should first reproduce in creation the tenderness of God's indwelling. God is so great that he can permit himself not to intrude. His presence in the world is powerful and at the same time so unobtrusive that we perceive it only by long practice. The more the Christian loves, the more unobtrusive he must

49

be. God's indwelling in creation also means taking part in life outside himself without expecting any return. Life, liveliness, feelings, the individual existence of the beloved should be assumed into our own life. Only the person capable of receiving gifts can really give love.

God spares no efforts

God comes and goes. He prepares for his coming. He preaches, gets tired, experiences human anguish, is nailed to the cross, appears in different forms and sends his Holy Spirit. In all this his intention is not to dazzle us with his divine power. In the elements, in plants, in fruits, in human beings who give us their friendship and understanding, in all these gifts God himself spares no effort on our behalf.

And the Christian of today should come to resemble the God who spares no effort, is in anguish on our behalf and seeks us out in all our ways. Often in human dealings the genuine expression of love is *caring*. God wills that humility and readiness to render service should be constant characteristics of the Christian, that the sufferings of the beloved should flow into him, and that the fate of the world should become that of the Christian.

God comes down to us

We see clearly in God a readiness to come down into all that is small and lowly in creation. That is why he willed to come down into the life of an unknown person from Nazareth.

50

For the Christian of today this attitude means that only a person rooted in God can hold firm as a lover in the difficulties of life. In a confused world he alone will put into practice the crystal clearness of all that is human and everything to which the word kindness can be applied. He alone, in a world of self-righteousness, can live humbly before the Absolute, live in true holiness. He alone can practise in all walks of life the attitude we call 'mercy'—and maintain it. All this will be lived out by the contemporary Christian only if he implores God's grace.

All the beauties of the world, but also all the cares of the world, find their home in a person who practises, by his life as a creature, this attitude of God's love for us. These things will not prevent his being at the service of love, even if he is the only one and is completely alone. He will sense that he can do nothing greater for the world than lose himself in God and nothing greater for God than give himself wholeheartedly to God's creatures, taking upon himself all their joy and all their distress. So the man who loves gradually becomes single-hearted, he embraces mankind, creation in its past and future life, in its painful hopes and in its longing for fulfilment. He can discover the invisible in what is visible. In such a person God's strength and driving force are given free scope in the world. God grips the world through him and creates in it its new being.

Someone might say that here we have given no practical advice or instruction to help in everyday life. But appearances are deceptive. The person who puts these demands of love into practice can say of himself that he has at least translated into reality something of that attitude which is the essence of Christ's life.

Future of Christian thought

Is there then a future for Christian thought? Our answer would be that it is possible, given certain provisos, for basic Christian thought to prevail in our lives in the future. What are these provisos? We must be cautious in our answer, for on it the future of Christianity largely depends. We name four conditions which we think essential.

Beauty

The first basic condition of Christian thought in general is that we should be fascinated by truth as beauty. It is certainly not just the truth of what we believe that affects us, but also its beauty. Hans Urs von Balthasar has insistently made this point in his excellent book, *Herrlichkeit*. In the thoughts of Gabriel Marcel also, the expression '*grâce*' means on the one hand 'grace' and on the other 'beauty' (perhaps with a shade of difference of meaning as in the Italian '*grazie*'). Christian thought should emphasise what constitutes a victory over the ugliness of the world. This would provide consideration for our teaching in the future, teaching valid not only for Christians but also for everyone else. This is a task for Christian thinking. Is our truth beautiful? If so, we should present it as such. If not, our thinking is in vain. Christian thought that bears no witness to beauty has no future.

Inner depths

Christian thinking should always begin in the depths of our being. In biblical revelation man's thoughts stem from the heart. His thoughts come up to the surface from his inner depths. Man's reflection about what is important originates in his heart. Clearly, a Christian is not called upon to speak about every mystery nor to present everything with the same emphasis. He has a right to deepen his acquaintance with the mystery to which he feels a special call from God. When he talks about this, it will be *his* grace-ful theology, his special charism, the 'theology of his heart'. We might say to a Christian: 'Go deeply into that truth for which you would give your life. But avoid trying to defend Christian theology or to triumph over others.' The Christian must assume an attitude of expecting nothing in return. Christian thought which does not come from the heart has no future.

Integrity

In the realm of our thoughts the upright man is one who does not pass judgment; he is open and ready to listen. Upright people can, however, become a menace to us. They view us with a searching, testing eye. They are certainly merciful towards the stupid, but merciless towards stupidity. An upright man often thinks slowly. He is conscious that he knows little and that of that little he has worked out the truth of a very small portion. That is why he allows himself and others time for a maturing process. The Church herself recognises, by an attitude of integrity, that baptism is an ongoing process. Christian thought not characterised by integrity has no future.

Assimilation
If one's thoughts come from the depths of one's being, one must enter upon an inner relationship with each of the truths meditated on. An assimilation of thoughts has to take place. Meditative thought, inner quiet and also prayer will often be needed for this assimilation. The Christian thinker must repeatedly ask himself: 'If this statement is true how can I go on living as I have done?' or 'What are the consequences of this for my own life?' or even 'How can I put this truth into practice?' If we are endeavouring to prepare a future for Christian thought we must at all costs reflect that the language of honesty is the only one in which God can communicate with a Christian. We cannot just take Christian truth for a stroll and chat about it for a while under a tree and then, at the appropriate time, leave it there and do something else. Christian thought is always making demands on us. Christian thought that is not assimilated has no future.

Here we should like to point out something which may be helpful. There is no real crisis in the Church. There are certainly questions and unresolved problems. But we consider it frivolous and irresponsible to speak of a crisis. Incautious talk about the dangers of schism and heresy might easily cause Christians to be affected by a contaminated atmosphere. Then there is suddenly a lack of consistency between one's words and one's attitude. One is left powerless. When a society lets this kind of thing go on, disaster may result from a mere chance event. We should therefore be grateful to all who radiate peace today and whose attitude makes things appear in their right proportions. We should be grateful to everyone who discerns the absurdity of certain assumptions and accepts life with clear-sightedness. The people of God gather round people such as these. In their company we can breathe freely.

Such people stand—and we should recognise this—between the two front lines. They are the 'third strength' of the Church. They are in our midst as peacemakers. Perhaps one day their work will be forgotten or claimed by others as their own. But they are guided by a delicacy, above all a striving for beauty, for inner depths, for integrity and assimilation of Christian truth. It is thanks to them that the atmosphere in our Church is purified. The present situation in the Church makes humility an obligation for us. If we try to practise it, we are already showing forth something of what God really is. The man who lives in humility is entitled to say of himself that his life has a future and that his thought is 'thought for the future'. Perhaps he can also affirm that his God is indeed a great and noble Lord.

2   In Practice

In the first part of this book I have tried to outline an honest programme for a good Christian life. Now we have to ask ourselves whether we can make this outline a reality in actual Christian living. Perhaps this can be done by practising the 'corporal works of mercy'. If so, Christian teaching is referring us back to simplicity of life: the essence of Christianity is 'love of one's neighbour'.

Love of our neighbour demands above all *feeding the hungry*. Wherever there is genuine human presence, the sign of the Eucharist is present, food for man—not only feeding with our bread but also with the nourishment of our own lives, our concrete existence.

Love of our neighbour also means *giving drink to the thirsty*. This includes, over and above the simple action of giving someone a drink, listening to the voice of those who can no longer put their needs into words. We must say aloud to the person who is lonely: 'My friend, you are not alone.'

A further concrete means of helping is to *clothe the naked*. Here too the contemporary Christian, in addition to the concrete act of clothing, should find out who is 'naked' in our world—surely those who are unmasked, shivering and threatened. This nakedness

57

will one day be clad with an eternal garment, when our mortality puts on immortality.

Further, Christian love of our neighbour tells us to *shelter the stranger*. Basically, everyone is a stranger in this world. Even Christians are by their very nature homeless. An offer of shelter to those who are materially homeless is one of the greatest and most important works of mercy.

Love of our neighbour also bids us *free the prisoner*. We are all prisoners, each in a different way. There have been certain times in history when Christians allowed themselves to be sold in order to free others from slavery. This is an important sign of what our inner attitude should be.

Christian mercy is also shown by the person who *visits the sick*. In so doing he should reflect that it is the visitor who really receives a gift. It is the sick person who gives the visitor the grace to be discreet and eminently merciful. It is the visitor's duty to show the sick person that our human nature is raised up to God's own mercy.

Finally, it is also an act of Christian mercy to *bury the dead*. The death of one we love can become—beyond the suffering that is uppermost—a gift of God to us. The Christian should try to recall all that was good and beautiful in the life of the dead person and all the possibilities with which he was faced. In this way he will bury in his own life the one who is dead.

In these seven corporal works of mercy Christianity opens up to us the dimensions and demands of

Christian love; without them we cannot live as Christians. If all Christians were to live according to these demands there would be less affliction in our world, less rejection and above all much less hatred. We must not allow help for those in corporal need to be the preserve of non-Christians.

How does one become a genuine Christian? We want to sketch a preliminary answer and develop it later. We shall do this first by considering the seven corporal works of mercy, then the seven spiritual works of mercy and finally reflecting on the ideal of the genuine Christian as outlined by Christ himself in what are usually called the eight Beatitudes. The separate sections are intended as food for thought; they call for personal practice and are really understood only by such practice. They presume no philosophical or theological background, only a heart that is 'ill at ease'. People who feel satisfied with themselves should steer clear of these chapters: they were not written with such folk in mind. How does one become a genuine Christian? We might give a tentative, and yet a very sound, answer: by the *corporal works of mercy*.

Feeding the hungry

Basically, Christ equated love of one's neighbour with the love of God. In the description of the judgment Christ even·gave love of one's neighbour as the unique criterion for admission to the kingdom of God. Everything else, however excellent and important, even knowledge of God and faith, is counted as an extra. Even martyrdom means nothing in comparison with love of one's neighbour. 'I may even give my body to be burnt, but if I have no love, I am none the better' (1 Cor. 13, 3). So we can conclude that beside *love of one's neighbour* all else pales into insignificance. When Christianity withdraws from the pressing duties of love for one's neighbour (i.e. the poor, the abandoned and those in despair), it has renounced its very essence.

But who is the neighbour that we as Christians must help in order to be worthy of the name of Christian? When Christ was asked this, he did not give an abstract answer but told the parable of the Good Samaritan. The lesson of this parable might be worded as follows: my neighbour is the person who has only me to help him. My neighbour is that person who will not be helped by anyone if I do not do it. So the parable is also saying: always be prepared, train yourself to be open-hearted, be sensitive towards suffering. Then one day you will meet a person who has nobody except yourself. By the love of one's neighbour we mean quite simply: *feeding the hungry.*

In this Christian challenge, concrete, physical hunger is envisaged as the object of beneficent love of one's neighbour. This hunger of the world is familiar enough to us today. But there is also in this demand the idea of an inner attitude, that of self-giving. Not only our works, but above all we ourselves, our being, should be nourishment for others. This is how we make the *Eucharistic attitude* of Jesus Christ a reality. In the Eucharist the person of Christ became totally present for others. Wherever one experiences what is genuinely human, the sign of the Eucharist, nourishment of people with one's own life, takes place. The Eucharist is—certainly not as an exclusive viewpoint but nevertheless an additional viewpoint—the openhandedness of one's personal life. This complementary view of the Eucharist enables us to see the Sacrament of Encounter as extending beyond the Mass itself, in certain circumstances beyond Catholic circles and indeed beyond Christian circles. Everyone can even now share in the Eucharist insofar as he gives his presence to the other without expecting any return, to the other who is, humanly speaking, completely broken. In so doing he makes the life-attitude of Christ a reality.

How the individual perseveres in this suggestion and practises it in his own life, and in other ways, only he can discover. But this will make him *a member of the Church*, a human being, who contributes something irreplaceable to the Eucharist of life. As Paul says: 'This is my way of helping to complete, in my poor human flesh, the full tale of Christ's affliction still to be endured' (Col. 1, 24). Through this unique contribution, unique because no one else can make it, a person becomes a genuine Christian.

Giving drink to the thirsty

The second of the corporal works of mercy is that of giving drink to the thirsty. This is a reality that guides us to genuine Christianity.

At last we can be honest

When Christ promised us the principle of witness, the Spirit, he added: 'When he (the Comforter) comes, he will confute the world, and show where wrong and right (and judgment) lie' (John 16, 8). What strange comfort! The Spirit of God is to show where right and wrong lie? All this means, however, is an inner setting-free. At last, in the knowledge of our own failings, we see clearly. We know where we are. At last we can be completely honest. There is real sin in our lives and not merely something ambiguous described by expressions like 'weakness' and 'guilt'. So there is something in our lives that we have to account for before God with regret. It is through the working of the Holy Spirit that a person begins to recognise his sins and to be sorry for them. Through the Holy Spirit a person no longer wanders around in the desert of his own failings, but returns to the source of forgiveness. Let us now ask another question.

Who is thirsty in our world?

We hardly ever hear of people being thirsty. What can a person say to us if he feels only the barrenness of his own life, of his own failure? To the Christian who is ready to help, to every Christian and not just to the priest, Christ promised 'an inner spring always welling up for eternal life' (John 4, 15). On the cross, in the desert of human despair, Christ himself uttered the cry made by many: 'I thirst' (John 19, 28). In our opinion, giving drink to the thirsty means listening to the voice of those who are incapable of *giving expression to their distress.*

If we listen, it may be that the other person will have the feeling that someone is at hand to help, even though in his own life he is unsure of himself, sinful and plagued by doubts. And this someone leads him back to the spring of mercy. Perhaps he cannot give an answer. But even his nearness is a help; it is soothing and refreshing.

By his words 'You are not alone', he brings fresh hope, but such consolation is not given without heavy cost to himself. This person does not counter the 'yes' of the other by a 'no'. He does not agree with him if he cannot do so. He does not let a thing be done if it would constitute a wrong. His gift is unequivocal. And suddenly the springs begin to bubble. A freshness of youth emerges from the sufferer's heart. New life comes into being where previously there was only the barrenness of the desert. He has found freedom. At last he has discovered a home in a human heart and seen a glimmer of hope.

A helping hand
A person living in despair calls for help from time to

time. The unexpected may then happen: someone, possibly one who is broken himself, is suddenly there near him, reaching out a helping hand to him. Suddenly his chains fall off. Meaning comes into his life. We wonder how this other man finds the courage to open up his life to our needs, to rise above his own misery and take on the burden of our difficulties. How does a person, himself broken, dare to help another? How can he hear our quiet, hoarse voice? How can he wish to make things easier for us? The answer is simple. His words 'You are not alone' are said and repeated again and again, in all loyalty, in the darkness of our existence.

Daring to help
Daring to help has always been experienced by mankind as an 'act of God', as an intervention of absolute Goodness in the darkness of the world, a darkness seen as the privileged place for experiencing God. This darkness is surrounded with a halo of the miraculous seen in the gesture of human help. The miraculous may be explained simply as human life in all its darkness and confusion taken up into the goodness of God. At no time in our lives are we completely lost and abandoned.

This knowledge, or perhaps we should say, this inkling, is the basic wonder of our lives, the unexpected, surpassing all hope. Now we see the fundamental structure of our Christian life. When you find *your way to your neighbour* you will become a real human being and at the same time you will find God. Whether this way to our neighbour is giving a glass of water or the more subtle listening to the voice of inner thirst, it is always a selfless action revealing the goodness of God.

Clothing the naked

A naked life is one that is 'unmasked', shivering with cold and threatened. Here are three points for our concrete work of mercy.

Unmasked
The worst degradation of man takes place if he is unmasked or 'shown up'. Our inner life—it may be the most precious thing in life or it may be something that, in our shame, we wish to hide—is brought out into the open and discussed. One then feels lost and stripped. Gossip obliges us to prevaricate. So our life becomes self-estrangement. If a person equates himself with his life, as it is discussed, he is lost. We ought to realise that the depths of life are so mysterious and bear the impress of so many motives, joys and worries that often a person does not himself know what is going on inside him. If someone in the goodness of his heart, without passing judgment, approaches us reverently, we feel 'clothed' and protected by his goodwill. We can once more

65

become what we really are in our hearts. By 'clothing the naked' we mean trying to understand them from within, not forcing them to put on an act and thereby become self-estranged. We mean respecting their secrets and refusing to allow unmasking to take place. No one should be unmasked in the presence of a Christian.

Shivering with cold

Nakedness makes one shiver with cold. Incidentally, the Church sees one of the fruits of the Holy Spirit as 'warming our hearts of snow'. If a person experiences too much reticence around him, too much coldness, it begins to penetrate his heart, makes him hard and cold and disturbs his natural cheerfulness. If we want to restore hope to such a life—now grown cold—we must cautiously, very gradually, give small tokens of kindness that will touch his heart and then 'his blood will begin to circulate' and his nature will regain its cheerfulness. Christian mercy demands of us that no one in our presence should shiver with cold.

Threatened

We sometimes say that a person has escaped misfortune 'with his bare life'. But let us also remember that everyone has only got his 'bare life'. There is not much else there. It is a very small remnant that we have saved out of the whole of our lives. Not much will be added to it. Pleasant, important events perhaps. Probably nothing essential. Job complained: 'Naked I came from the womb, naked I shall return whence I came' (Job 1, 21). But our life will be clad in an *eternal garment.* It will be clad in its exterior nakedness by God's mercy. 'This perishable being must be clothed with immortality, and what is mortal must be clothed with immortality' (1 Cor. 15, 53). Clothing the naked means showing forth the transitory state of our world in the perspective of heaven, fostering in our hearts the thought of the resurrection and of heaven. Much could be said on this subject; for example, what Christ understood by 'garment' and how a person was cured by touching the hem of his garment. Anyone who reflects carefully on this will discover something of importance. We suggest for meditation the following passages: Matt. 9, 20; 17, 2; 22, 11; John 19, 23; Rev. 1, 13; 7, 9–14; Luke 15, 22. The reader will be able to find other passages for himself. The one fact that emerges from this meditation is that Christ thought of giving *personal help.* He did not think so readily of organisations— even though they do much good and are often more Christian than we are. It was something very personal that he had in mind. His programme was intended to show forth the living presence of God in the world: it was carried out almost entirely in a person-to-person situation.

Breakthrough
When we unselfishly show our approval of the life of another, we give him courage. We do not look beyond the present to a Utopia but try to give fresh vigour to his

life and make a breakthrough out of his hopeless situation. We take pains to think for others, lighten their burden, assess their situation and pave a way for them. It is astounding to see how life flourishes if one inspires a person with confidence and 'clothes' his life with goodwill. Quietly and unobtrusively we can show by our friendliness that people are kind, good and lovable, and that the qualities of which they give promise only need an opportunity for them to be developed.

Sheltering the stranger

'Being a stranger in need'—a condition painfully experienced by so many in our times—rightly makes one stop and think. A human being is *always on his way to somewhere else*. We can understand him, according to our ideas, as stray, tramp, traveller or pilgrim. Here the image of 'way' is not synonymous with making for a goal, but often represents a fruitless attempt to find any goal at all. Current philosophy of human life has come back to the Christian thought of *pilgrimage*. It is characteristic of a human being that 'he has never arrived, he is always waiting' (E. Bloch); our ways are only rough tracks which suddenly come to an end in discomfort (M. Heidegger); so our life is not just waiting but, even more radically, 'expectation consisting of expectations which themselves await expectations' (J-P. Sartre); accordingly, 'hope is the raw material of which we are made' (G. Marcel). All these statements merely illustrate the definition of human life expressed earlier by B. Pascal: 'we are not yet, we hope to be'.

Challenge
This experience, reaching to the very fibre of our being, is perhaps the greatest grace of our times. It is a vital challenge to Christian holiness today: to offer a home and inner peace to the person who has strayed and is lost in loneliness. In this context we must emphasise the urgency of *giving serious consideration* to the term 'foreigner'. English people are instinctively given a jolt by the word foreigner. The foreigner is really foreign to us. His habits, his attitude to life, his whole manner of thinking and his life-style are different from ours. His attitude to us and his reactions are unfamiliar or difficult to fathom. Even his God is unknown to us. Therefore he is a person we mistrust, whom we do not immediately feel inclined to make welcome among us. We offer him a *home* because Christ has identified himself with him. In so doing we feel our own personal sense of isolation. The foreigner is only the personification of our situation, our inner homelessness, our lack of security, our anxiety, our feeling of strangeness. The longing for a final home grows out of our offering him a home. We should be grateful to this stranger. He has made a gift to us, not vice versa. The refugee has in one way or another been uprooted. He is literally an uprooted man. He has not only been driven

69

from one country to another but also from one language to another. Suddenly he finds himself condemned to live without friends and acquaintances, to express himself in a language which he has not completely mastered. His escape has brought anxiety with it and even now he often feels that people are 'after him'. Perhaps he may settle in a corner of some town and have the feeling that everything is strange and that the world exists only for others. He has to get papers and wait in corridors for residence and labour permits. These problems, it is true, are to be solved at administrative and 'welfare' levels. But there remains a final duty for our personal Christian action: we must try to offer the refugee a fresh *sense of security*. Genuine human help must come into the picture—and this is a Christian action. By our friendship we can give the foreigner a new home. He should realise that he is not living in hostile surroundings, that he has friends who think of him and who do not laugh when he mispronounces a word. By letting a person who is homeless share our own lives we save his life. A generous heart is the Christian solution for a person who is homeless. We would even suggest that our eternal salvation depends on the help we offer to the stranger, the outcast and the refugee. At the moment of death Christ will come to meet us and say: 'Come to me, for I was a stranger and you took me in, you made friends with me.'

Setting prisoners free

Let us begin with a brief introduction to this subject: Christ told us clearly and unambiguously that we visit him in every prisoner. There have been times in the history of the Church—determined, it is true, by social conditions, yet revealing the depths of Christian reflection—when Christians sold themselves to free others from slavery. External imprisonment may itself be an expression of *inner freedom*. The fact that Christ was bound and imprisoned before his death was a symbol of his restricted and unsuccessful life. By its suffering he gave to this life its final meaning of inner freedom. What happened once and for all in Christ's life is repeated daily in our lives: freedom in spite of *constraints*.

We are all prisoners, each in a different way. Life itself holds us enchained. Our aims, our obligations, our life's task freely taken upon ourselves, these are only a small portion of the reality that we might have been. The inclinations gradually formed in us, our friendships and our love—all these circumscribe the horizon of our lives to a certain extent. Our fulfilment is only partial. Our hearts cling to what we have and what we are capable of. And so our life is closed to other, perhaps more wonderful possibilities. Worry, humiliation and *despair* enslave us to the monotony of the daily grind. Our own body is often a prison. We notice this only when it begins to threaten and cramp our mind. And in the depths of our lives we are fettered by something uncanny which we call sin, which is contrary to our nature and yet almost unconquerable.

In the Purgatory of Dante's *Divine Comedy* there is a description of human imprisonment which strikes home. In the external visions an inner panorama of life is revealed, a place of punishment. Man reaches upwards and waits for redemption. 'Then I saw a noble company gazing upwards in silence, pale, humble, as if they were waiting.' Man must 'climb up' seven steps to reach final deliverance. Each step signifies a level of interior purification. The transition from one 'terrace' to another involves great effort. The nearer one gets to the top, the easier the climb. Not because the way is easier but because one becomes more heavenly.

The *transformation* is effected in this manner: first, pride is atoned for and humility acquired; then envy is overcome and unselfishness practised; interior harshness is changed into gentleness; inertia gives way to joyous activity; we are freed from covetousness and our life becomes characterised by generosity; what is inordinate is rectified and self-control is learnt; lust is purified by penance. Could anyone have given a more complete account of deliverance from human constraints?

So, setting prisoners free means living our lives as a witness for others, to show that it is possible even now, in our earthly captivity, to cultivate *longing for freedom*, to live in that attitude which is a condition of our entry into Paradise: 'From now on do not wait for a word or a sign. Your will is now free, upright and holy and it would be a sin not to follow it. So I make you your own ruler and pope.' During our life we should become an *angel of hope* for our neighbour, a messenger from God, capable of bursting open the fortress of his life, so carefully bolted and barred, as was Peter's prison. A man who has inner freedom—a man of wisdom—is not more knowledgeable than others, but he is certainly more ready to overlook things. He is kindly disposed towards what is done to no purpose and sympathetic towards what is extravagant. With the suspicion of a smile he notices how life is played out and spent, how it remains poised and gathered in upon itself as a coiled spring until it is once more set free and can find its own direction. The man thus freed guards one of the most precious and rarest secrets in the world and he, in his turn, is guarded by it: God's patience with creation. He endures what is imperfect, he is lenient towards what is faulty, he treats failure with an unobtrusive caring which amounts not only to mercy but also to a feeling of hidden solidarity in face of the same fate.

Visiting the sick

To be ill means, in addition to confusion, suffering and depression, waiting for someone, like the sick man at the mysterious pool in Jerusalem who lay there for a long time suffering and waiting until, in the end, someone passed by and took pity on him (John 5, 1–16).

The unexpected day
His waiting lasted thirty-eight years. Year after year the sick man saw the waters moved and others restored to health. He often tried by his own efforts to slip down into the water. He had already put pressure on so many people by his begging. Then—expectedly or unexpectedly—came the great day for which he had given up hope, when he could tell a human being of the deepest suffering there is, the suffering underlying his life-long illness: 'I have no one'. There was no reproach or bitterness in these words, just a lament and hopelessness.

The sick man brings us a grace
By our visit we probably cannot heal the sick person or lessen his pain. But there is one thing we can do: tell him—possibly without words, merely by our silence and our presence—that he brings us a grace, that the world would be unthinkable and no longer bearable without the support of a life of suffering.

Visiting the sick
Christ descended into the abyss of human needs. Even in suffering, or precisely through suffering, the transformation of the world into the reality of the God-man is accomplished. It is one of the greatest graces of visits to the sick that we can witness to the world Christ's attitude of hope, expressed in the words of the second letter to the Corinthians: 'It is you I want, not your money' (2 Cor. 12, 14).

74

What happens during a visit to the sick?

Our friend who was ill lay before us. We did not dare to move; we sat there motionless and at the same time held his life in our hands. Then we began to bear his illness and his suffering in ourselves. The world was contracted to the dimensions of the small room where we bore the suffering of our friend. As we felt it we thought of something that later we could not or dared not explain to anyone. In our human sympathy the eternity of God's mercy came to life. Our human mercy became for us an experience of God, the proof that there is a God of infinite mercy.

There is a God

The important question we have so often secretly asked ourselves and sought in vain to answer is: If there is suffering, how can there be a God? This was suddenly changed by this experience: could we imagine a God at all if our friend were not suffering there before us? Our silent compassion became a revelation of God.

Hopelessness

It was because our request could not be answered in worldly terms and because our human love, brought to him in friendship, seemed so futile that God's mercy could be put into words. And it occurred to us that we had spoken words of lamentation not in an empty space but to God.

The mysticism of human help
This experience is so fragile, it takes place so close to the borders of mysticism that any further attempt at explanation must be a failure. We can only hint at the experience of which Augustine of Hippo once spoke.

In worldly terms nothing can be explained
Augustine said: 'Let me speak of your mercy. It really is *to your mercy* that I am speaking. It is not to a man who would laugh at me.' Every noble human deed, every sign of sympathy and every question, every struggle to find meaning and cause, to cope with suffering and need, would strike a strange note if there were only this world, people and the sphere of human beings. In purely worldly terms our life is a prey to something strange. But human experience at its deepest level shows that *nowhere in our life are we completely lost and abandoned*, for we live from the beginning in the heart of God. We can make our compassion for a sick person an occasion for self-revelation of God, an opportunity for a ray of hope. We have a victorious weapon against despair, the simple words that we should keep repeating: 'God is greater than our heart' (1 John 3, 20).

Burying the dead

In human life there is such a thing as 'friendship with the dead', with people whom we have lost. It is very painful. Christ himself experienced this pain when his friend Lazarus died.

Christ's pain at the time of his friend's death

The death of Lazarus entered mysteriously into Christ's life. Writing of this death John the apostle spoke of the 'glory of the Son of God' (John 11, 4). The death of someone we love can become, beyond the suffering that is uppermost, a gift from God. The dead person is already enjoying the protection of God's mercy.

But what happens to us?

It helps us to think of the good and beautiful things the dead person did during his life and of the possibilities still before him when he died; it is good for us to make his life present to ourselves and to do this repeatedly. *A Witness before Death* written by Dietrich Bonhoeffer at Christmas 1942 for his fellow-conspirators says:

> We are not Christ, but if we wish to be Christians it means that we ought to have a share in the breadth of Christ's heart by responsible actions which freely seize upon the present moment and expose us to danger, but also establish a solidarity with all our fellow-sufferers—not in fear but in the freeing and redeeming love of Christ. Passive waiting and apathetic looking-on are not Christian attitudes. A Christian is not moved in the first place by what he experiences but by what his brother experiences. Christ has suffered for him in deed and in sympathy.

We need to clarify one point: surely this corporal work of mercy ought to bring us some measure of consolation? In various publications we have already outlined the following view of *death as final decision*.

Not until human death takes place are we offered the possibility of making our first fully human act. In death we find consciousness, freedom, encounter with Christ and decision concerning our eternal destiny. Only at the moment of death can man give up the freedom of his own life. Only in death will he have sufficient self-mastery to be capable of meeting Christ fully, with all the fibre of his being, and of making a final personal decision. At the moment of death we should be able to assume for the first time a fully personal attitude. You might ask: Is not such a view of death over-optimistic? Or if, at the hour of death we still have the final possibility of deciding, why need we hurry to begin now to live a Christian life? I give the following answer to this objection.

Life as conversion

Who and what gives me the certainty that I shall make the right decision at the moment of death? The result of this last decision depends on me alone. There is no other norm by which to measure the sincerity of my wish for conversion except conversion itself. At this present moment of my earthly life I must begin now to be what I want to be in the future. I must make use of the many small decisions during my life here and now if I sincerely wish for conversion at death. I ought not to live thoughtlessly and leave everything to the last decision. Who can guarantee that at the end I shall change the direction of my life? The thought of a possible final decision at death does not in any way lessen our need to be watchful with regard to salvation—quite the contrary.

Spiritual conversion
In seven reflections we have considered the seven corporal works of mercy. New dimensions have been shown us. But if we wish to answer realistically for our actions in a way that gives us hope, we *must* take into account the sum-total of the demands that Christ makes on us. These demands include the spiritual works of mercy dealt with in the next section. In his dealings with those who are merciful the Christian himself grows and sees how new horizons of hope are opened up by Christian action and how a person can enter into the needs of his neighbour by bearing his sufferings with him.

3   Future Prospects

The spiritual works of mercy carry Christ's demands to a degree well-nigh impossible of attainment. They open up to us perspectives of a possible future.

A 'man of the Spirit' can perform the difficult service of admonishing sinners and bringing them back to a state of sorrow for sin. This must be done delicately, not harshly, so that no rift arises between the one admonishing and the one admonished. He can also instruct the ignorant and guide them into God's presence, not by killing the idea of God by pompous talk but by helping them to be clear about God's way of acting.

A Christian should not condemn the doubting person whom he counsels. Everyone has some kind of doubt. A Christian should prevent his neighbour's doubts from turning to despair. In consoling the afflicted a Christian must avoid mere edifying and stereotyped lectures but be prepared to spend time with the afflicted. His presence should result in a relationship often difficult and exhausting for himself; this is what is meant by faithfulness.

We do not always bear witness in words; silence, too, can often be an answer that rings true. This is Christ's demand: that we suffer injustice patiently. Christ, in

80

forgiving those who insulted him, by his example turned human values upside down. He showed us that God, in spite of rebellion and disobedience on the part of man, always remains faithful. The Christian should strive for such surpassing forgiveness and thus be Christ's witness in our contemporary world.

Finally, the Christian has a duty to pray to God for the living and the dead. His prayer should be directed above all to this most important request: 'I beg of you, my God, to let these people for whom I pray learn that you really are Love itself.' These are inner attitudes which will be outlined here. They show us that a genuine future will not be fashioned from without, but chiefly from within.

Admonishing sinners

Among the spiritual works of mercy the one that takes precedence over all the others is a particularly difficult service, that of admonishing sinners. A spiritual person is invited to open up fresh horizons of forgiveness for his neighbour. Christianity has had its 'spiritual persons' from the very beginning. They form an essential part of the Church. In a certain sense every Christian is a spiritual person, for each of us will be called upon sooner or later to lighten, by spiritual works of mercy, the sufferings of our neighbour. It is hard to say to one's neighbour: 'If you go on like this, your life will fall to pieces!' At the same time it is also a *kindness that inspires hope.*

The neighbour must at some time or other strive to 'come clean' with God and with himself. This will happen if he submits to the searching look of God's love and utters the words: 'God, be gracious to me, a sinner!' When by sorrow a man sets himself free from the poison that is killing his soul, he can joyfully go forward towards a new future. Repentance is not a virtue of the weak, it gives proof of *inner greatness*. It was the saints—men of unfailing inner vigour, lighting up the world by their strength, goodness and purity—who spent their lives in repentance and self-denial. Repentance shows that a person is sympathetic towards what is new, different and better, that he can remove the evil lurking in his heart and make a completely fresh beginning.

A *new spirit is awakened* in a repentant heart by brotherly admonition. Good advice need cause no rift between Christians because both the one advising and the one advised feel they are sinners. As far as their sinfulness is concerned, there is no difference between them. But there is a difference in the insight and sincerity with which individuals regard their sins before God. This difference is clarified by a mysterious event which occurred during the crucifixion. Both the criminals crucified with Christ were sinners. Both rebelled against the man dying with them and they abused him. But then, in the violence of his pain, a *mysterious transformation* caused one of them to reprove his companion and beg Christ to think of him in his kingdom. By this avowal the criminal was rescued from the futility of his own sin and the hopelessness of his suffering. Not so the other. Both were in the same situation, both had to suffer death on a cross. There is no difference in the circumstances. But the one found an inner freedom, the other remained obdurate and closed (by this we do not mean to pronounce on the eternal salvation of the so-called 'bad thief'). It is not granted to all of us to experience to the full what weighs down and threatens our neighbour and to bear in ourselves his inner disorder. In many cases this would break us.

For this reason the Christian needs *to be careful* if he reproves others. The apostle Paul gave us this advice: 'Brothers, if a man should do something wrong, on a sudden impulse, you who are endowed with the Spirit must set him right again very gently. Look to yourself, each one of you: you may be tempted too' (Gal. 6, 1). For this reason it is not possible to draw up any general rules as to how a Christian should reprove. Each one must discover before God when, how and for whom he might be the person 'to lead someone home', and where he can open up a future of fresh hope for his neighbour. When conversion has come about, a *new future* is open for this neighbour and he can then concern himself with the complete divergence between good and evil. The past is bound to continue to influence human life to a certain extent. But in the domain of all that is personal, where man is truly himself, all is changed. And even our sinful past, which has stamped our psyche, takes on a new meaning and a different significance. In the light of fresh promises the person begins to control his past life. In this way he brings about a deeply-rooted turning towards all that is good.

Instructing the ignorant

The gloomy mystery of our times is often described as the 'darkness of God'. How, at such a time, is one to instruct the ignorant? Unwittingly we have all become ignorant. In any case this darkness of God cannot be counteracted, today less than ever, by a secret theological language. What takes place today can be explained only by the harsh expression 'attempt to suppress God'. To begin with, we need to be conscious of this situation. Only then can we say a few words about the spiritual work of mercy, instructing the ignorant.

Killing the idea of God by pompous talk
When we speak about God we often use meaningless formulas, empty concepts, big words and fallacious statements. Contact with atheists is for many believing Christians boring precisely because they are always talking about God. This kind of talk ought to die out (and will) if it does not come from the heart, if the person has the name of God only on his lips. The old formula used in theological training that 'inner understanding makes a true theologian' is still valid in our

day. A Christian will convince no one by mental acrobatics. It is by loving God that he bears witness to the mystery of God's love. It is a sign of hope that the younger generation of Christians no longer accepts the God of our pompous talk.

The anonymous God

Where the Christian's heart is, there, in reality, is his God. For the believer there is never a 'God in himself' but always only the 'God I experience', the 'God of my life'. This God is all that is most intimate, hidden and essential in individual human destiny. And so in our lives as Christians a purer and nobler image of God should be formed ever more clearly, beginning with our tiny, intermittent and confused experiences of God and growing into a here-and-now process of encounter. Wherever the God of our life is present with greater intensity, a new way is opened up for us so that we have sufficient light at least for the next step. The God who is not approached and who has therefore become anonymous is not a 'God for human beings'.

The God of our life does not make us speechless, he is not someone of whom we cannot talk and who has no name. Even when all names fail, the name our love has given him and the name we repeat with an endless number of changes is 'my Beloved'. The God of whom we speak pompously, the anonymous God, is also a *distant God*. In the Bible the distant God is always called the 'God of the godless': 'To God they say, "leave us alone:"' (Job 21, 14). When the Bible speaks of the fear of God, it is only because God humbles the proud and disturbs their self-righteousness. In Psalm 10 the word 'arrogant' is contrasted with 'poor'. The proud and arrogant are those who hunt down the poor and oppress the unfortunate. God leaves them alone. On the other hand: 'Thou hast heard the lament of the humble, O Lord, and art attentive to their heart's desire' (Ps. 10, 17). The wicked come to grief at the hand of the 'God of the poor'. For a man who recognises and confesses his inner misery God is the most High. For him God is also the overwhelming image of the fulfilment of all his longings. Such an image of God is justified because there is still much in us that is humanly unfulfilled; it is justified too when man has the courage to confess his frailty.

There is one further reflection. A man who is poor of heart takes God for granted and finds him the greatest source of enlightenment. It is part of the nature of the mystery of God that he bestows his presence only on the person who has reached the innermost heart of revelation. When this happens, God reveals himself to our neighbour, who can then instruct the ignorant. God's truth, instruction of the ignorant, can be carried out only in a framework where these factors are present. The God who is close to us, the God of our life, the living Beloved of our longings, cannot be the object of abstract proofs but is always and only the Beloved to whom we witness. Where one is really concerned with the living God, irrelevant talk is bound to cease. Even accurate and conclusive thought will be changed into challenge. The essence of what we mean by instructing the ignorant is concealed within a life that bears witness to the God we experience.

Counselling the doubtful

The demand made on the Christian to counsel the doubtful must never be construed as condemning doubt. To doubt is not to be opposed to God. As people in search of God we all spend our lives at risk and in uncertainty. Whether this lack of clarity in life appears as darkness or even abandonment by God, it would be a basic misunderstanding to regard it as a threat to faith.

We all have doubts

No Christian, young or old, believer or not, tested or as yet untested, should refuse to admit that he has doubts, whatever the reason and whatever the kind. Moreover, he is a doubter who has not finished with his doubts nor will he do so in the future. He might as well dispute the fact that he is a wretched sinner, or at best a sinner rescued from the fire. But, faced with doubt, the Christian should not despair: that is the last thing he should do because in today's conditions of salvation his doubt may be an essential element of his faith.

Faith often means that doubts have been overcome. The prayer of many a Christian is 'I have faith, help me where faith falls short' (Mark 9, 24). So a Christian should not be horrified by his doubts concerning faith and should not define them as atheism. They may well belong to the maturing process of the Christian life. God's command to us to counsel the doubtful by our generous and understanding attitude means that we must try to prevent our neighbour's doubts from· turning to *despair*. How can we do this? If we are to counsel contemporary man successfully, if we wish to hinder his doubts from changing to despair, then we must take them seriously. Doubt often shows how much nonsense we still hold on to in our supposed faith. Doubt often urges us further forwards. It gives us a jolt and attacks our indolence. We should not expect everything at once from a person who has doubts. It is enough for him to assent to the *essence of faith* if he feels influenced by the purity and uprightness of Christ, if he has admiration for the grandeur of the life Christ makes possible for him. The essence of faith is not so much a matter of reasoned formulas. Perhaps the doubter has nothing to say on the level of basic intention. So much ingenuousness, lack of depth, deviousness in our reasons, easy by-passing of the reality may prevent the doubter from seeing eye to eye with the Church's concrete statements; at a deep level he often recognises the importance of Christ and the significance of the Church as supported by the mind and heart of Christ. Therefore we should give prominence to the concept of *global acceptance*. We do not attempt to discover if this basic inclination to believe can find its appropriate expression in systematic dogma, definitions and statements. It is possible to be a genuine Christian, to assent to the basic truth of Christianity and still in many—even dogmatic—questions, defer acceptance. In spite of lack of decision in detail a man's global acceptance of Christ may be vigorous, and with it the eventual decision to go right along the way he shows to the end.

In doubt one may, and should, peacefully postpone acceptance. Uncertainty and inability to accept immediately are sometimes genuine steps on the road to belief. One can hold fast to the basic truth of revelation and practise it even if one has only a partial understanding of the consequences and cannot as yet regard these consequences as truth to be lived out.

Concretely, what is our idea of a *Christian counsellor*? Augustine of Hippo once described the basic attitude of a Christian giving counsel to a person in doubt as follows:

> Those who do not know what sighs and tears even the least knowledge of God costs may be angry with you. Those who have never been led astray may be impatient. But I cannot be angry with you. Let us search together for what is unknown to all of us alike. Not one of us should be so bold or so conceited as to think that he already possesses the fulness of truth. Allow me—this I can ask of you—to listen to you so that I can then talk to you.

Augustine has here said the most important things about counselling the doubtful.

Comforting the sorrowful

Mercy means readiness to enter into complete union with a person who is suffering. At the same time it means the will to endure loyally, in union of heart, with the sufferer. Both qualities make a breakthrough in comforting the sorrowful.

Union of heart
A Christian who consoles only 'from outside' and makes edifying and stereotyped remarks to the sufferer may make his state worse, he may even bring him to rebellion. The sufferer feels that such consolation is a mockery: 'You say all this because you have no idea how deep my sorrow is, because my suffering is not yours. You would have a right to console me if you were suffering as I am, or if at least you could suffer with me!' The comforter of the sorrowful must himself be sad. If then he can speak words of comfort, they no longer come from without but from within. The language of consolation can be accepted only if there is union of hearts. Then there is no longer just *the* suffering of which one speaks, but *your* suffering which through our mutual love has become *my* suffering. It often suffices for a Christian who loves a sorrowful person just to look at him and stay unobtrusively beside him. Because of the presence of someone affectionate the sorrow ceases to wear him out. He finds a support in life. The world about him has been changed. He is no longer enclosed in the narrow confines of his hopeless

situation. The comforter has opened a new world for the one in sorrow and has roused him to a fresh life, although perhaps nothing is changed in his exterior condition. This is 'creative presence'; here genuine consolation is given.

Faithfulness

The person who dares to console in this way must also take upon himself the consequences of his surrender, must really console faithfully by practising this creative presence again and again; this means that a difficult and exhausting relationship is formed, and this is what we mean by being loyal and faithful. We do not take upon ourselves the suffering of the other if we bear it with him just once. If we do this we are not consoling him, we are deceiving him and making his suffering worse. Consolation that is loyal and faithful demands great endurance, selflessness and affection and, above all, much patience. The most faithful people are also the most humble. We should realise that the *duty of consoling* is a grace. In the help given by the comforter to the one in sorrow the comforter himself experiences consolation. Paul said:

> Praise be to the God and Father of our Lord Jesus Christ, the all-merciful Father, the God whose consolation never fails us! He comforts us in all our troubles, so that we may in turn be able to comfort others in any trouble of theirs and to share with them the consolation we ourselves receive from God. (2 Cor. 1, 3–4)

Often, life without consolation finds God out of reach

so that we, fragile human beings, are the sole comfort for the sorrowful. Often the one in sorrow can no longer pray. In the fairy story, *The Snow Queen*, Hans Andersen describes how completely lost little Kay feels because his life has gone cold: 'He wanted to say the Our Father but could only remember his multiplication tables.' In this situation the Christian is called upon to allow the person who is lonely to *share in his own consolation*.

The Christian has no right to keep for himself the consolation he receives from God; he must let it overflow to others (cf. 2 Cor. 7, 4). What would be the use of a Christian life if someone near us had to complain: 'Reproach has broken my heart, my shame and dishonour are past hope; I looked for consolation and received none, for comfort and did not find any' (Ps. 69, 20). In order to remain in an attitude of readiness to offer consolation the Christian must often forgo human recognition.

We end by mentioning a final quality of comforting. It should be carried out with *tenderness*. The Bible writes very simply of God as comforter, and the Christian should be his representative for his neighbour: 'As a mother comforts her son, so will I myself comfort you' (Is. 66, 13). Tenderness is not weakness or something to be undervalued, it is an ability to show affection which knows how to shield the most lovable things in the world and to treat them with delicacy and reserve.

Bearing wrongs patiently

It is not always by our words that we bear witness. Silence can often be a real response. It is a strange thing that the one who suffers in silence is often thought to be right. We prove by our silence that the truth is in what we are rather than in what we say, and people can even be won over by silence. The patience God requires of us is the generosity which does not let anger, even righteous anger, turn into a second evil, which does not let evil beget evil. One becomes a Christian when one knows how to 'head off' powers of destruction, when one tries to sort things out and to become clear-sighted, silent and ready to serve without becoming impatient. Perhaps no one will thank us for being peacemakers. But God will 'credit' us with this and pardon much on account of it. We want to write briefly of two examples from the life of Jesus where wrongs were patiently borne: his silence before Pilate and before Herod.

Jesus' silence before Pilate

'Jesus refused to answer Pilate one word, to the Governor's astonishment' (see Matt. 27, 14). Pilate was most probably a well-educated man. But when he said to Jesus 'What is truth?' he did so, not as if he were ill at ease and searching, but with resigned apathy. This showed how confused he was. He was bearing responsibility but did not know for what purpose or for what reason. It is possible in our world for a man to do as he wills with human beings; that such a person is

93

apparently successful brings to light the dreadful state of our world. The world that grows up around such a man is deceitful, a place where it does not pay to commit oneself to a cause. What is essential becomes of no account; the truth becomes unimportant and man is a cultured nobody. In a world such as this there was no opportunity at all for Jesus, who said of himself that he had come to bear witness to the truth, that he was *the* truth. He accepted his death sentence in silence. He really had nothing to say to Pilate. Jesus patiently bore the wrong inflicted on him.

Jesus' silence before Herod

'Jesus gave Herod no answer' (Luke 23, 9). Jesus seemed even more powerless before another powerful man, Herod Antipas, into whose hands fate had delivered him. Herod obviously had no idea of what was meant by human dignity. He was certainly a pathetic individual for whom anything exciting, spectacular and out of the ordinary was of interest. He was therefore delighted when Jesus was sent to him for 'he had long been wanting to see him and had been hoping to see some miracle performed by him' (Luke 23, 8). Herod was demanding of Jesus what entertains many and helps them to overcome the monotony of life. In Herod's presence Jesus did nothing and did not say a single word. He could not do or say anything without betraying his fellow men. Herod really said to him: 'You're here for me; you interest me insofar as you prove that you can please me—have a try: perhaps we shall get on well together.' What happened with Herod is just like what happens with many human beings today; and everyone who realises he is a person feels it to be a deadly insult. 'Then Herod and his troops treated him with contempt and ridicule and sent him back to Pilate dressed in a gorgeous robe' (Luke 23, 11). Here too Jesus showed how wrongs can be borne patiently.

The *fate of Jesus* came to grief in these events and at the hands of these two powerful men, Pilate and Herod, who clearly had no conception of the highest values in life, of truth and reverence. At the hands of such men the fate of many a human being comes to grief. Christ lived out to the last extreme what many of us experience at one time or another in our lives.

The mind and heart of Christ

A final determination to be a human being, and to remain a human being in face of all the injustice which presses on us, is suffering wrongs patiently and is, ultimately, imitation of the mind and heart of Christ. The one who believes this can still bring hope to our world.

Forgiving injuries

What is meant in a Christian context by the expression 'forgiving'? A Christian may say: 'You were weak, I understand you; we won't think any more about your

95

frailty.' We believe that Christian forgiveness is essentially more than this. Christ never defined forgiving in the sense that he *forgot* injuries. They just no longer existed. There was no suppressed feeling of insult lurking in some dark corner of the soul. *Christian forgiveness* means obliterating the worst about our neighbour, not only from our memory but from our heart; not to act 'as though it had never happened', but to testify that for us 'nothing happened'. Peter experienced forgiveness like this when Jesus looked at him: a fresh hope of being allowed to go forward. Then Peter went away and wept bitterly. This set him free and opened up a new future with God.

Transformation of values

This shows us what Christ was really concerned about. Christ is not the answer to questions of politics, social structures, literature and the use of leisure. Men must accept their own responsibilities for such things. They must search for solutions and explore possibilities. God has given us enough reason and discernment to rule the world. No redeemer is needed for this. But where a man is broken under the burden of his own guilt, under the burden of having insulted God—politics, literature and philosophy are of no use at all. Then only God can provide us with an answer. If he does not give it we are lost. But he does give it as he gave it to the good thief on the cross: *Today you will be with me in Paradise.* The fact that we have been well-mannered and respectable all our lives does not count with Jesus. What he wants is our heart, not respectability, not a marvellous career. The heart of a criminal is eternally of value to him. In the last minute we must say 'yes' to him. Then all is well.

There is hope for us all

When a person has understood the words of Jesus to the good thief and then lets himself be influenced by human regulations and arrangements and powers, he cannot be helped. Even the criminal has the same hopes as we have. If we do not want to accept this, we are pushing Christ himself out of the world and holding on to our own ridiculous regulations.

Quick! Get up!

Men bound this criminal in chains. For him there was no further possibility of escape. But God entered into the prison of his life and spoke to him as the angel did to Peter: 'Quick! Get up!' But the poor man could not do this now. He obeyed Christ and so went to heaven where, even with his feet in chains, he could still make his way. He went out of our world with its calculations, reprisals and sheer decorum. Anyone who has dreamt of a radical revolution can see in this how revolution is brought about: by forgiveness and by thus giving hope to those who have no hopes left. But the word of final forgiveness was spoken by the one who was himself nailed to the cross.

Divine extravagance

We can see the kind of forgiveness God demands of us when we look at salvation history, that history in which God has first lived out his own pardon. In salvation history we discover a mysterious set of laws that we might call the 'law of divine extravagance'. Right through the Bible we notice that God outlines his plan for salvation and, when man thwarts this plan, God makes of the thwarting itself a way out for a new and nobler plan for his grace. God remains faithful despite man's rebellion and disobedience. God's will is un-changeable—as unchangeable as love which does not permit of deviation or withdrawal, but builds everything, even withdrawal, into a still greater in-centive to love. To such radical, extravagant pardon God wishes to guide us so that we keep the world on the right path.

Praying for the living and the dead

What does it mean to pray for the living and the dead? To turn to someone who is available for all alike, who embraces every sphere of life, who has mercy on everyone? Prayer is an exchange of life between friends who feel that their destiny is interrelated. No creature stands alone before God. A man knows that in prayer he stands before God with his fellow human beings. The place therefore, where, at the deepest level, creatures are together for one another is no other than before God. In God, as in the depths of one's being, the creature finds the Beloved. Love for a human loved one suffers no limits. It is the norm of everything. When we look at God our finite affection becomes absolute surrender and love.

How is man to pray?

To come nearer to an answer let us take two of the many examples in the New Testament. They are perhaps the most important texts for the meaning of prayer of petition.

Asking with simplicity

> When you pray, go into a room by yourself, shut the door, and pray to your Father who is there in the secret place; and your Father who sees what is secret will reward you. In your prayers do not go babbling on like the heathen, who imagine the more they say the more likely they are to be heard. Do not imitate them. Your Father knows what your needs are before you ask him'. (Matt. 6, 6–8).

When you pray, do it simply and naturally so that it may be free from all self-seeking and hypocrisy. Here the room is a symbol opposed to the 'street'. When you pray, do not be eloquent. Do not think that God is dependent on the number or kind of words you use. Your words are really superfluous, and yet God wants them—but with due modesty. You must pray and at the same time you must know that he sees what you need better than you do. If you ask from the viewpoint of his knowledge, your prayer will take on a form pleasing to Christ: you must speak to God but be aware that he knows your words before you speak. You stand there naked before God who knows your innermost thoughts.

Ask with the assurance of faith

'Whatever you ask in prayer, believe that you have received it and it will be yours' (Mark 11, 24). This is the second and perhaps more important text. Here it is a question of the assurance of faith in prayer of petition. It is formulated as only Mark can formulate. He uses three tenses all mixed up together. The request (present), the receiving (past) and the granting (future). We must hold fast to the original reading. Here is an echo of the great words of the Lord in Isaiah: 'Before they call to me, I will answer' (Is. 65, 24). That these words of Jesus do not exclude insistence in petition is shown in the general Gospel tradition, above all the tradition of solitary, labouring prayer throughout the night.

What shall we ask for?

What in a Christian context is the meaning of petition? We often feel our helplessness before the affliction of our fellow men. We see how life, death and, above all, the fate of those we care for are threatened by wickedness in the world. With the spontaneity of his love man calls on God to avert these threats. At the same time the man who prays knows that he would be basically ungodly if he harnessed his God to earthly well-being. So the one who prays sincerely leaves the

100

outcome to God's discretion. Our prayer should be directed towards the granting of one thing: 'I beg of you, my God, to let this person for whom I am praying, whether he is alive or dead, know that you are really Love. Let this insight dawn on him in spite of all the affliction of his present and future destiny. Let him really know that his final refuge is in you and that all his hopelessness is well cared for in your love.'

Only love counts
The deepest prayer does not reach out for help in each individual situation but for God's grace for an inner transformation so that we understand life in a new way, with fresh eyes. For the person who understands this the request made never results in disappointment, but always gives true enlightenment.

I should like to end this whole section on the spiritual works of mercy with the words concerning our desires in prayer that Christ addressed to Saint Mechtilde of Hackeborn. They apply equally to our desire for prayer. 'I will accept your love, not as it is in you, but as if it were really as great as you long for it to be.'

4 The Complete Christian

The so-called 'eight Beatitudes' basically contain, concisely expressed, the sum-total of Christ's promises for our Christian, indeed for our human life. The demands they make are certainly hard but it is equally certain that they are intended to help us to find happiness. Until one has prayed much and has had long experience of affliction and much joy, one cannot grasp the essence of real happiness.

We need to understand something of the meaning of the eight Beatitudes: inner poverty—which does not necessarily exclude temporal possessions—leads to joy; it is part of our happiness to be present and grieve with those who are in distress; spiritual greatness is shown in the struggle for courage to be gentle; it is good and right to endure hunger and thirst after righteousness; the joy of living requires us to be the witnesses of God's mercy in our world; everyone who is pure of heart and can see God is blessed; it is essential to be a peace maker if one is to be happy. Finally, it contributes to our joy if we are persecuted—in whatever way—by those who do not understand these demands or do not wish to understand them.

Fundamentally, a man knows that it is not by

thoughtless drifting through life that he builds up an existence characterised by maturity and the happiness that goes with it. But it is important for us to receive from Christ, clearly and without misunderstandings, the assurance of such knowledge. We learn that Christ is truly the 'God of our heart'. The demands that Christ makes are at the same time promises; they are blessings or beatitudes.

Poverty of spirit

What is really meant by happiness? To answer this question we must refer to the description given by Jesus Christ in the eight Beatitudes. He speaks first of *poverty of spirit*.

What is meant by poverty of spirit?
It is given as the first basic condition of happiness because in it—insofar as it is not just material deprivation but rather an inner attitude—is fulfilled that fundamental decision when a person ceases to equate his own person with having things at his disposal. He is saying: *I 'am' more than all I 'have'*—'I am more than what I have gained or acquired at any time'. By this statement, which is really a decision, a breakthrough to freedom takes place. The person no longer allows his life to be restricted by anything. He does not allow his way into the unknown to be barred by things he acquires. He is more than all he has at-

103

tained, achieved, striven for and experienced in this life. A feeling of inner relaxation is born in him.

No one can take from me what is really mine
'I can, with legitimate energy and freedom from anxiety, move on towards greater things without allowing myself to become attached to anything whatsoever either in myself or in the world. I can let everything make claims on me. I can spend time calmly admiring the beauty of the world but I can also be present with people in their anxieties and distress.' Basically, poverty of spirit is the *openness of a heart that loves.*

When a man is open in this way it is more or less a matter of indifference to him whether his life is successful or not. He lets what is shallow and superficial in things pass him by. He is ready to listen, he does not push himself forward and he is free from self. In this way he overcomes force of habit, apathy and all that is trivial. He frees himself from 'being stuck in a rut', allows his impulses to go their way and is open to a present moment that is ever new. The first, instinctive impulse of a man who is thus relaxed is an *unobtrusive goodwill* towards life, people and events—instead of an eagerness to gain possessions. This becomes a creative ability to hold fast when his sympathy is not reciprocated or when it is misjudged or rejected. His inner relaxation inclines him to turn inwards and be recollected. It enables him to look out on a new world. The person wants things for their own sake, in their original nature, which he respects. He does not want things first and foremost for his own use. He can spend time with a person and remain there with his eyes and heart wide open.

He does not possess the world . . .
. . . yet the world yields up its innermost character to him, something more than all possessions. The upshot is a relaxed existence with a vision and knowledge in depth. People are prepared to tell all their secrets to a person whose life is like this because they know that they will not be used or abused, manipulated or placed in situations of expediency and know-how foreign to them, but accepted as unique in their joys and afflictions. A new world grows up round such a life, the result of an attitude of self-surrender: it is the realm of all that is unique, sheltered, recognised and safeguarded. When Jesus Christ said 'How happy are the poor in spirit; theirs is the kingdom of heaven' (Matt. 5, 3), he spoke of the first condition for happiness.

It should be possible to outline a Christian view of a human being according to the basic principles of the Sermon on the Mount, especially the eight Beatitudes. There Jesus Christ gave his portrait of a real human being. The time has come for our Christian thought to develop a picture of a human being from the totality of Christian experience in the sense of Paul's words: 'You belong to Christ, and Christ to God' (1 Cor. 3, 23). In the following sections I want to undertake this venture

105

of fresh Christian thinking. However, it suffices at this stage to open up new dimensions and to indicate fresh possibilities.

Sorrow

The attitude of freeing ourselves from selfishness which, in the last paragraph, we called poverty of spirit, enables a person to be at one with another human being. This does not merely mean a special ability to have the same feelings but—beyond that—an ability to *share in what happens to the other.* Such a person feels drawn especially to lives that are crushed and humiliated, to people who can no longer escape from their painful misfortunes. Shyly and without thought of reward the person is open to the need of the other and offers him a home within himself. Faced with the suffering of the other, he keeps silence but he is totally welcoming to human frailty. He invites the 'poor, the crippled, the lame and the blind' to share his feast and his fellowship (Luke 14, 12–14). He feels he must *break out of his own human home* and personally 'have nowhere to lay his head' (Matt. 8, 20), so that he remains continually ready to be with the oppressed. It is a joy for him no longer to be his own master, to share the rejection of others, to make his own life common and ordinary and to grow rich by his self-sacrifice.

A man like this, attracted by the needs of his neighbour, does not approach the one who is suffering *in the attitude of an adviser*, as an outside helper and sympathiser, but actually becomes part of the person of the sufferer. Here it is not only fraternal aid and charitable action that are at work. All this may be part of it, and should be, if a heart ready to help is to prove its value. But the dominant attitude goes deeper, to self-dispossession, to that 'more' of love which makes us willing to let our life be overclouded by the darkness of the suffering of the other. We cling to the one we love in a hopeless destiny, we endure the hopelessness of our neighbour and enter into the humiliation of a broken life, not in sentimentality or emotion, but because of an attitude to life that has come to be our own mind and heart. This is a sorrow which, in its darkness, surrounds every selfless lover in the bleak, lonely, comfortless and often fruitless world of human destiny threatened by suffering and death. The inner disconsolateness of such grief can exhaust a life and make it hollow and bleak. The person thus becomes insecure, weary and full of anguish. And yet he keeps rallying again, *offering to be present* once more even when he is no longer understood by many. The essential action of such a person is to abandon himself to the grief of the world. The experience is nonetheless decisive and of far-reaching significance for an understanding of Christian life. Gradually, in a slow process of faithfulness and long-suffering, such people build up an inner core far removed from all the fortuitousness of moods or of arguments that hit the headlines or of apparent disappointments.

Here, in the centre of life, a new dimension of real consolation grows up: *the happiness of no longer belonging to oneself*, of self-dispossession, of inner surrender. These people live, in the essentials of their lives, already secretly 'on the other side'. Thence they receive again and again the strength calmly to let themselves be used, without show or self-pity. They have already 'disappeared' out of this world. We can see only the traces of their greatness in the consolation we receive in what happens to us: 'Happy are those who mourn: they shall be comforted' (Matt. 5, 4).

The happiness of those who mourn is self-contained and cannot be referred to something more important. But if we could speak of this happiness we should have found a new language. We have all already had experience of such moments of happiness. They have made the inner, abiding happiness of our life transparent. It was a matter of just 'being there' for our neighbour in intimate contact and complete openness. The event itself is often indescribable, yet undeniable for the one who has had such experiences in his life. Happiness in sorrow! What a mystery, but one so intimately connected with all of us!

Gentleness

Poverty of spirit, readiness to be unselfish, if honestly practised, changes our life into a determination to open our heart in sorrow to the distress of the world. By this a new core in life is formed in the Christian, a delicacy of attitude towards life. This special form of stability amid the contradictions and the confusion of the world might be called *courage for meekness* or gentleness. It is certainly not the virtue of the weak but of those who have an inner strength and do not find it necessary to give tit for tat or to hit back. This, however, is only the negative side of meekness. Its positive side consists in a basic affection for the human being in his confusion, an affection which a person shows with delicacy for those who are a threat to him personally.

Obviously, this meekness is also expressed in other forms—as an attitude of reserve, leaving others free and not forcing them, of not 'setting oneself up as someone', of peace in one's look and recognition, of refinement of speech and a certain distinction. It is in love for one's enemy that it is best proved and shown in all its purity. It does not mean a cowardly condonation of what amounts to evil. It does not mean either that the person will cease to defend what is just and true, what is lovable and worthy of value, and what is vigorous, when confronted by an attack on the part of a sinful person. In other words, he will not permit a blurring of the frontiers and an explaining-away of objections.

Love of one's enemy is in no way artificial, but natural, a primeval impulse of every affectionate person. The person is really saying: *I do not look upon you as an enemy*. What this means is: 'There may be plenty of opposition between us. If I defend myself against the evil that you propose to do me, it is not out of enmity that I do so. I do not want to win a victory over you, or to humiliate you. I do not wish you any harm at all. I will not even assert myself against you. I do not hate you, I even feel that you are in the greatest need of my love because there is so much that separates us.' Without this fundamental inclusion of the person of the enemy in one's affections the Christian cannot attain that peaceful recollection which is a preliminary condition of happiness. His heart will be poisoned by thoughts, feelings and plans of hatred and rejection. His conscience cannot become free: negatively biassed, it becomes unreal and materialistic, the slave of the person hated and even the slave of the hatred directed against himself. This is the worst sense of loss that can befall a person: insofar as he remains in this state he can possess nothing in peace, accept nothing without worry and he cannot surrender fully to beauty, truth and fulfilling love. He can no longer remain close to the world, no longer 'inherit' the earth.

On the other hand, love for one's enemy is *the highest affirmation of freedom a human being can make*. It shows his view of the world and his over-whelming greatness. To be in the company of such a one is a great blessing. At the same time his work among us is to abolish hatred. His influence over the heart of man is powerful because it is completely in-ward, his goodness attracts. A person of this kind can really become a 'shepherd of souls', even a 'shepherd for life'. People quite involuntarily seek refuge with

110

him. Our life itself is open to him. In the company of such a person no suffering is involved. 'Happy the gentle: they shall have the earth for their inheritance' (Matt. 5, 5).

Jesus and gentleness

In the Gospels the unselfishness of Jesus appears most clearly in his gentleness. This was perhaps the heart of his message. Behind the outward manifestation of his gentleness (for example, when he shielded sinners from the so-called righteous, children from the Apostles, Mary from Martha and from Judas) an inner freedom is to be seen. This man, Jesus, unlike us, had no need of hostility to incite him to work for freedom. By his very nature Jesus Christ had no enemies at all. This is what he demanded from all honest Christians. Only in this way can we be open and completely unbiassed.

Hunger and thirst after righteousness

Hitherto we have spoken of three essential conditions of Christian happiness: poverty of spirit, sorrow and gentleness. A *just world* is brought about in the presence of people possessed of these qualities. It is a type of life where a person is firmly established in his own person, at home with himself, in a realm of existence where everything is in harmony in a new order of being. The life of such a person becomes, for a human being, a 'place to settle'. Beside him there is no

111

need for shame or pretence. One can be really good without fear of being exploited. One can be one's real self without experiencing violence and destruction of this inner harmony. One can show one's inner kingdom, be kind, *without arousing envy*, without becoming a laughing-stock. One can be true, good, kind, unique and so find continual fulfilment.

The feeling of being 'at home' is what is meant by Isaiah in his 'indescribable description':

> Then the wolf shall live with the sheep, and the leopard lie down with the kid; the calf and the young lion shall grow up together, and a little child shall lead them; the cow and the bear shall be friends, and their young shall lie down together. The lion shall eat straw like cattle; the infant shall play over the hole of the cobra, and the young child dance over the viper's nest. They shall not hurt or destroy in all my holy mountain; for as the waters fill the sea, so shall the land be filled with the knowledge of the Lord.' (Is. 11, 6–9)

The truth of these verses lies not only in the *description of peace*, superabundance, beauty and clarity but also in the impossibility of what is said, in the incompatibility involved in the description. The 'right order of things', a life where one feels at home, is at one and the same time the most beautiful and the most difficult goal of our longings. It is given to us only in 'endurance'. It is concentrated occasionally in particularly unselfish, open, gentle people and also in groups, communities, in those who long for such conditions in the world. Their longing bears within it *fulfilment as promise*.

There is an undercurrent in the history of mankind:

the trend of those who yearn, those 'who have nothing', who know that they are hopelessly poor, hungry and deprived in all they do. They are lowly people but their eternal longing for eventual fulfilment persists. And although they have yearned for so long, although they have sacrificed so much, shed so much heart's blood and have still been repeatedly disappointed, cheated and deceived, they still cannot bring themselves to cease to understand or hope any longer. Why? I think it is the inner experience of their longing itself, the *presence of fulfilment in the longing*, the presence of what is longed for as an essential element in human longing, the inner experience of the 'attainment of the unattainable', a direct insight into the words of Christ: 'Happy those who hunger and thirst for what is right: they shall be satisfied' (Matt. 5, 6).

God means 'taking risks'
We must face one fact: 'hungering and thirsting' in human life repeatedly means taking risks. Justice is a risk of this kind. There are people who pray at length and very earnestly and yet have never been shocked in the depths of their heart by the injustice in the world. Man is given nothing that should fall to his lot according to human justice—not even justice in the world. The return of the Church to the service of mankind, to the struggle for justice, is the same thing as belief in God and in Christ. By this we mean that we must associate with people, be attentive to them and even follow them in their extreme isolation, in order to

be with them as persons and so fight for justice. 'Go out', Christ said to us, not, 'Sit down and wait until someone ready to fight comes along!' If we were to practise Christ's demand for hunger and thirst after justice, Christendom might experience a new hour of grace here and now.

Mercy

Although we have already considered the works of mercy, the concept of mercy occurs again among the Beatitudes. Repeatedly Christ's teaching comes back clearly to this topic because it is central and very important.

Heartfelt sympathy in human affliction

A person full of longing and caught up in a yearning for greatness feels solidarity with those who are abandoned to lives that remain unfulfilled—not through condescension but because of a heartfelt sympathy with human affliction. There is, as it were, a secret bond between all those whose suffering is real, the common fate of those who are 'shown up' for what they are.

Can the world live without mercy?

It is the common fate of the hungry, the sorrowful, the thirsty, of those who are hounded and persecuted. It does not include those who make a virtue of their poverty, misery and hunger, who are content to be pious, enjoy this and make a show of it; those who make a lot of their affliction, who explain their illness as health, who pronounce their hunger to be satiety. Nor does it include those who run round wearing a mask behind which they hide their distorted faces. No one can live happily behind a mask.

We cry out in our longing for happiness

This longing makes us call out when we are hungry and in need of nourishment. The one who is thirsty asks for a drink. A life that is bleak and naked is icy-cold and wants to be clad. The foreigner or stranger looks for a door to be opened to him. The prisoner dreams of being set free. The sick person hopes for health and the wanderer for home. The ignorant person feels his limitations and asks for guidance. The one who is sad wants to be consoled. Injustice calls out for justice. The one who offends hopes for forgiveness. The whole throng of the living and those who are dead await anxiously the close intimacy of our friendship.

Who can provide for all this affliction?

Is it possible for a person who has never been hungry, or sick, or a stranger, deserted or abandoned and despairing, to understand all this affliction suffered by human beings and to offer them a home in his heart? Probably not. He may well go towards all of this with generosity and enthusiasm, want to take it on himself and try to bear it for others. But he will not succeed— not ultimately, *not where suffering becomes meaningless.* No one can take away from me my suffering, my sin, my loneliness. They are not stock-in-trade. Just as no one can take away my birth or my death, so no one can take away my misfortunes. But they can be alleviated by one who has himself experienced the meaninglessness of a suffering life, if he comes and sits beside me when I am sad and . . . does not even say a word. I shall feel that he is my friend who can do nothing better for me than share my sadness, and then I shall no longer be left alone in my sorrow.

Is there any meaning in such help?
This 'sitting beside me' would be completely senseless if he were not my friend. There is no other explanation for human consolation: we have become one. The only way he can express this union is by sympathetic silence. Perhaps answers and explanations fail him, but he does not wear a mask.

The God who redeems and sets free
The God who sets us free must come down and be with the 'unmasked' if he intends to be our friend, the friend of the lowly and the hopeless. His gift of himself to us, of himself emptied out, deserted, hungry, doomed to die, will be understood only by those who have the courage to become at one with the unfortunate, who themselves can sit down as a friend with all those who are abandoned.

116

God's mercy

Those who show mercy in this way will be aware of
God's mercy. Perhaps others will not notice Christ at
all, Christ, the inconspicuous man full of longing for
God, who said to us: 'Happy the merciful: they shall
have mercy shown them' (Matt. 5, 7). Without mercy
the world would be unbearable. 'You who are poor and
in want, you shall have life!' are words of mercy.

A pure heart

We have tried to describe the character of a man who is
happy by considering the central element of human joy
and the effects of not belonging to oneself. The man
who is poor in spirit goes with an open heart towards
things, events and people. He allows himself to be
claimed completely by human fate, even by sorrow. He
excludes nobody from a share in his affections and lets
gentleness prevail even with regard to his enemies.
There is a longing at work in him which stretches out
beyond pettiness to the promise of a just world. He
would like his friends too, those oppressed and in
anguish, to share in his happiness and therefore he tries
to soften their suffering by his selfless presence. We
sense *a new kind of existence*: being oneself in self-
sacrifice. Here is a person possessed of singleness of
heart, forgetfulness of self, limpidity: his life is transparent. Gradually everything that is cramping fades
out of it. An essential cheerfulness is characteristic of

him: joy and peace begin to prevail, generosity, patience and a simple friendliness develop. Peace and clarity surround him; his very nature becomes friendly. It is a strength full of mystery radiating from a pure heart. It is the *strength of beauty*.

It is not violence that moves and captivates us. It is not the grandeur of mighty mountains or stormy seas. It is the strength of what is bright, transparent, the light of a clear day or of a person who is fully mature. It is the strength of a person at one with himself, asking nothing of us, not imposing himself, giving all he possesses and happy withal. *We are captivated more by this witness of a pure heart* than by all the power in the world. Happiness, possibly the result of reflection, living for others, is here at work, a clear characteristic without any ambiguity. And if such a person is devoted to us we are deeply touched. His devotedness is complete and unconditional. We are tempted to say: 'No! You can't do this! I am not worthy of your devotedness!' And yet it happens quite naturally, just as a flower or a tree spreads out over us and yet remains pure and unsullied.

Such people ring true
Meeting them is one of the greatest graces of our life. Their openness and devotedness are a proof for us that they look through us into an eternity, into an absolute being, whose being is focused on us. They already see God and are with him in the thick of all the miseries of this world. 'Happy the pure in heart: they shall see God' (Matt. 5, 8). Such devotedness in purity *obliges*

118

God to enter into our world and give himself to it. This is also Mary's secret. 'When the time had come, when God resolved to realise his incarnation before our eyes, he had first of all to raise up in the world a virtue capable of drawing him as far as ourselves. . . . He created the Virgin Mary, that is to say, he called forth on earth a purity so great that, within this transparency, he would concentrate himself to the point of appearing as a child' (Pierre Teilhard de Chardin). In the Blessed Virgin the life of the universe was concentrated. She enabled Life, Jesus Christ, to come down, to lead us and the universe over into the final fulness of life.

Christ was a pure being on fire with love
The disciples experienced this transfiguration, this intensity of reality in a staggering manner: 'Then he was transfigured; his face shone like the sun, and his clothes became white as the light' (Matt. 17, 2). This passage gives us a glimpse into the life of one pure in heart and in such a person life could not fail to be a beacon of light.

Peace

Nowadays one of the most difficult problems for human deliberation, decision and (underlying these) unselfish love is establishing peace. People who are happy always have something creative about them. They establish, create something of holiness and grace

119

in our world. Peace is their most necessary task. It is an inconspicuous task. It is not a question of producing new elements in life, of creating fresh impulses and thoughts. Establishing peace comes from something already at hand, something which has grown disorderly and *has to be brought back into harmony*. It is basically a humble action which is nearly always forgotten or later claimed by someone else as his own. It is also something which calls for unobtrusiveness. In establishing peace one often goes unnoticed. One has to catch on to emotions, calm them down, sometimes let feelings clash and be relieved, and one has to look for solutions. Only a person who is firmly rooted in the truth can establish peace *without being insulting and also without compromising*. There is only one truth and that has to be brought into being.

Certainly today (at a time of increasing terrorism and disturbances of the peace on all sides) it is exceptionally difficult to preserve due proportion and find appropriate means. Establishing peace today sometimes demands persevering, well-considered and vigorous action. In spite of this it remains a task of selfless love intent on avoiding harm to anyone. Often the peacemaker must enter into the confusion of his opponents. But he must at the same time *preserve an inner clarity of vision*, stand firm and remain silent and at peace. Peace can be established only by one who has found inner peace in himself or whose life is spent searching for peace. But this peace lasts only an instant. The harmony laboriously built up threatens almost immediately to collapse. It therefore seems to me that *the God of peace must be at work* in a person who can radiate peace.

This 'God of peace' (2 Cor. 13, 11) who 'chose (through Christ) to reconcile the whole universe to himself, making peace through the shedding of his blood upon the cross' (cf. Col. 1, 20) wills at the same time to reconcile everything in heaven and on earth. Around the peacemaker is concentrated the transformation of our world, making it Christ-like, like God's Son, who is 'our peace' (Eph. 2, 14). This happens even if the peacemaker does not know, or fails to recognise Christ. People who make peace are sons of God. Some experience of their attitude is sufficient for us to catch a glimpse of Christ himself. 'Happy the peacemakers: they shall be called sons of God' (Matt. 5, 9). At times this establishing of peace calls for harsh words.

In plain words, concerning peace, Erasmus of Rotterdam wrote about the soldiers' Our Father:

> How can a soldier in a parade service say the Our Father? Shameless braggart! You dare to call on God as Father while you hold a knife at your brother's throat? Hallowed be thy name. How could God's name be dragged deeper in the mud than through your brawls? Thy kingdom come. You pray like this and at the same time establish your power by violence with streams of blood? Thy will be done on earth as it is in heaven. God wants peace. But aren't you preparing for war? You ask the Father of all for daily bread. But don't you nevertheless scorch and burn down the crops of your brother because you would rather perish in misery than let him have the use of them? How have you confidence to pray: Forgive us our trespasses as we forgive those who trespass against us while

121

you are planning the murder of your brother? By your prayer you want evil warded off from you. But aren't you trying to lure your brother into snares at the risk of his life? Don't you long to be delivered from evil while plotting the most shameful designs on your brother?

However, to be a Christian *one does not have to become a pacifist*. On the contrary one should attempt to engage one's enemies in conversation—a much harder thing. One should stand ready for action between the two fronts and persevere in waiting for negotiations to take place. A Christian should live out this spiritual attitude even when he has little apparent success.

Success

With this thought in mind we end our reflections by asking the question: How does one become a genuine Christian? We attempted to answer this important question by considering the seven corporal works of mercy, then the seven spiritual works of mercy. Finally we thought about the eight Beatitudes. Then we examined the *question of human happiness*. We did not look at our superficial wishes or impulses or our longings according to appearances, but at the deepest concepts of mature human existence, concepts which we have so often belied but can never really forget. Will the person whose attitude we have described *be successful in the world*?

Christ answered this last question: 'Happy those who are persecuted in the cause of right: theirs is the

122

kingdom of heaven' (Matt. 5, 10). He added significantly 'Happy are you when people abuse you and persecute you and speak all kinds of calumny against you on my account. Rejoice and be glad, for your reward will be great in heaven' (Matt. 5, 11–12). *What does this lack of success mean in the life of a Christian?* In these reflections we have been closely concerned with what it means to be a happy person. We were convinced by the evidence. At the same time we suspected too how much at risk such an existence must be. There is the inner suffering of a happy person, the cross which comes as a result of happiness. For there is no greater distress than to be happy within oneself and at the same time at the mercy of the hopelessness of the human condition. Yes, one can be both simultaneously.

Happiness and hopelessness

These two are not imposed, from without, on the person who is happy, but as he lives out his happiness they are his from the start. His happiness consists in the fact that he enters into the circle of those who have lost hope as one who shares honestly in their misfortune, in order to *bring about justice in the world*. The 'just world' is seen in the process of being realised in the life of a good man. It will not be established by magic but built up by human hands, through human suffering, supported by human faithfulness. Ever to be open to the mystery and rooted in the depths of all that is human (even in hopelessness) is what is meant by

123

happiness in a Christian context. What we have hitherto worked out about the happiness of mankind is covered fully and completely by the picture conjured up by deeply human concepts.

There is nothing new and surprising in the Beatitudes. *Everything in them is completely human* and corresponds to the fundamental form of human life. What is surprising is not that a human being can think, guess at and long for such things, but that a human being really succeeded in translating into reality in himself all these longings and concepts. This is what was outstanding in Christ's life. This is the goal of our efforts as Christians: *to translate into reality the mind and heart of Christ.*

At this point, with reference to Christian teaching concerning man, it might well be maintained that man himself—according to the somewhat sensational but apt title of the book by Alexis Carrel—remains *Man the Unknown* until a Christian scholar reflects basically about Christ and his teaching. *The one who forgets Christ has forgotten himself.* There is an unpleasant phenomenon called 'loss of memory'. It happened more than once in connection with the war. A person lives, does this and that, but has forgotten his real identity. The Christian should not be a person who has forgotten his own name. Again and again, in humble surrender to Christ, he should be able to repeat: 'It is good that you exist!'

Home to fortified desert castles,
Adorned with wall-paintings from floor to ceiling.
The largest mosque in the world
called Samarra its home,
I imagined that the call to prayer
reached me in the clouds.

Allí en el desierto hay fortalezas y castillos adornados con
pinturas enormes que van del techo al suelo. La mezquita
más grande del mundo eligió a Samara como su hogar.
Imaginé que la llamada al rezo llegaba hasta las nubes.

My cloak took me to Muslim Spain,
Where the East met the West.
I passed scientists, inventors
and court astronomers,
Testing the limits of human knowledge.

Mi capa me llevó hasta la España
musulmana donde se encuentran el Este y el Oeste.
Allí ví científicos, inventores y astrónomos reales
quienes llevaban al límite los
conocimientos humanos.

There, I wandered through ornamental courtyards,
Past fountains and scented gardens.

Atravesé patios ornamentales con fuentes y jardines perfumados.

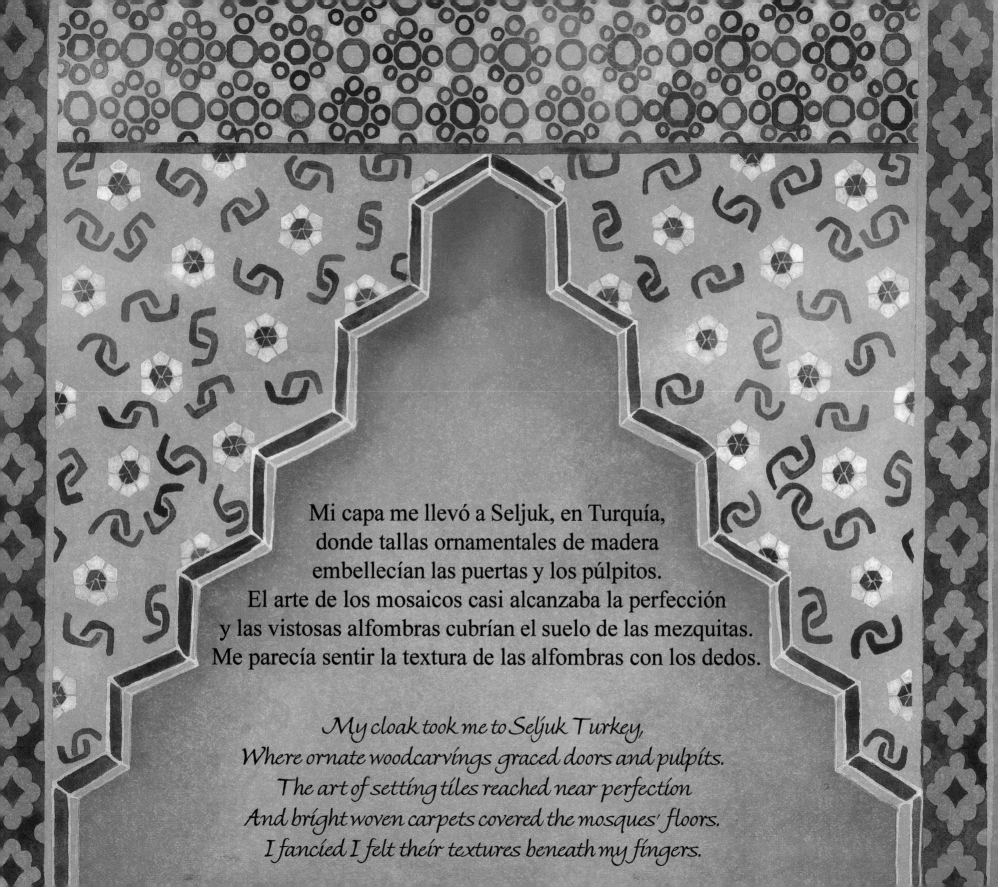

Mi capa me llevó a Seljuk, en Turquía,
donde tallas ornamentales de madera
embellecían las puertas y los púlpitos.
El arte de los mosaicos casi alcanzaba la perfección
y las vistosas alfombras cubrían el suelo de las mezquitas.
Me parecía sentir la textura de las alfombras con los dedos.

My cloak took me to Seljuk Turkey,
Where ornate woodcarvings graced doors and pulpits.
The art of setting tiles reached near perfection
And bright woven carpets covered the mosques' floors.
I fancied I felt their textures beneath my fingers.

Mi capa me llevó al
Tamerlán de Samarkand donde se
congregaban los artesanos de todo el mundo

*My cloak took me to the Samarkand
of Timur 'the Lame'
Where artisans from around the world
were gathered.*

Escultores de la India,
calígrafos de Persia,

Stonemasons from India,
calligraphers from Persia,

joyeros de Turquía y
tejedores de seda de Damasco.

Silversmiths from Turkey and
silk-weavers from Damascus.

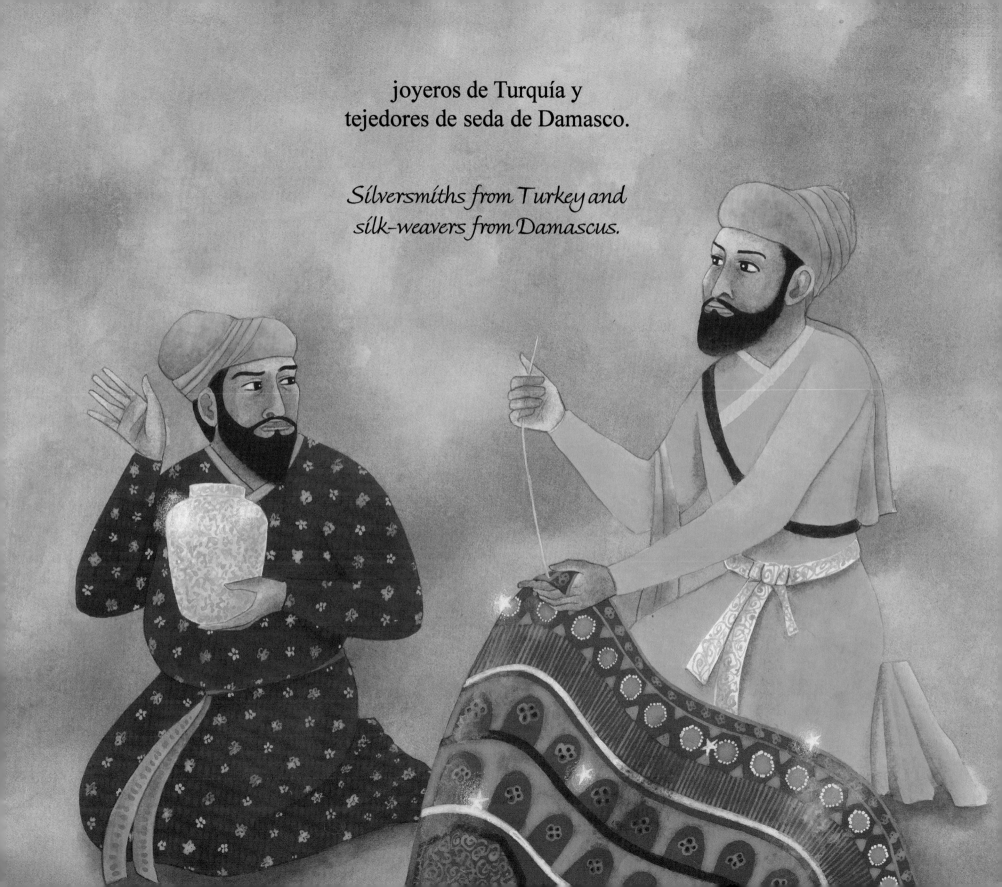

All brought back as captives, to beautify his city,
While his palace was a tent – a nomad to the end.

A todos los traía cautivos
para embellecer su ciudad
aunque él fue nómada y hasta el
final vivió en una tienda de campaña.

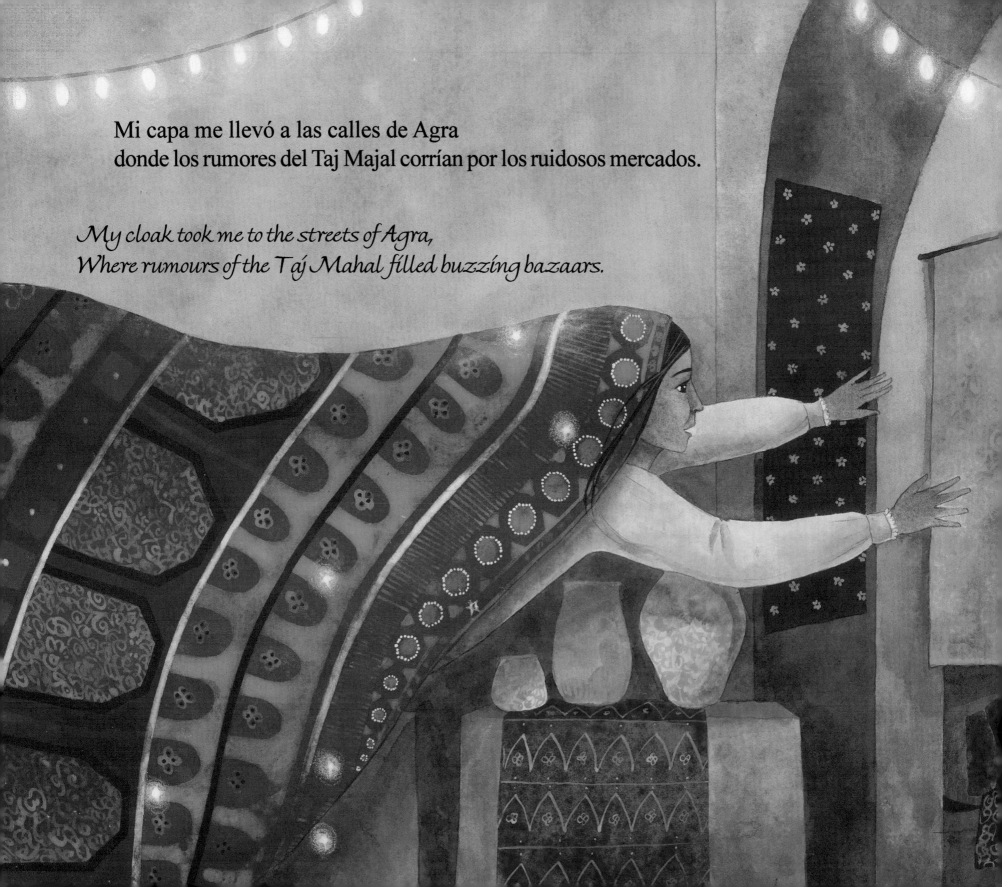

Mi capa me llevó a las calles de Agra
donde los rumores del Taj Majal corrían por los ruidosos mercados.

My cloak took me to the streets of Agra,
Where rumours of the Taj Mahal filled buzzing bazaars.

Un edificio originado en la promesa hecha a una moribunda y que,
cubierto de mármol blanco,
resplandece con la luz.

A building born from a deathbed promise,
Its garment of white marble
Shimmered in the light.

المشرق

Calligraphic inscriptions from the Qur'aan,
Floral arabesques and geometric designs
all harmonised
And the poets named her 'Dawn's bright face'.
I wished its beauty could grace the living
and not enshroud the dead.

صباح الفجر

Tiene inscripciones del Corán en caligrafía, arabescos floridos y diseños geométricos que se complementan armónicamente.
Los poetas le llamaron "La cara brillante del amanecer".
Yo quisiera que alegrara a los vivos y no sirviera de sudario a la muerte.

Este viaje fue sólo un sueño, la fantasía de una niña,
pero los lugares existen de verdad.
Espero que puedas tejerte una capa con este cuento
y visitar esos lugares tú también.

This voyage was a dream – a child's fantasy,
Though all its destinations are true.
I hope that your cloak will be spun by this tale
And that you will go there too.

Here are some explanations to help you enjoy the story:

Samarra
In the 9th century, after the foundation of Baghdad, the Caliph (ruler) moved his capital to the splendid city of Samarra. The Great Mosque was once the largest mosque in the Islamic world and rises to a height of 52 meters.

Islamic Spain was established in the 8th century by Muslims from North Africa who were known as Moors. For over three hundred years, Muslims, Christians and Jews lived together in a Golden Age when learning, art and culture flourished.

Seljuk Turkey was one of the eras in Islamic history. The Seljuks were Muslim rulers who took control of Persia and Turkey. Seljuk Turkey became the centre of excellence in weaving, ceramic painting and wood carving.

Born in the 14th century, **Timur 'the Lame'**, also known as Tamerlane, was a fierce and determined Mongol warrior who loved art. Whenever his armies invaded foreign cities, he would take care to protect the artisans and take them back to beautify his city, Samarkand.

The **Taj Mahal** was a monument built by the Mughal Emperor Shah Jahan in 1631 as a tribute to his loving wife Mumtaz Mahal. Legend says that she made him promise to build her a mausoleum more beautiful than any the world had ever seen.

Arabesque is an art form originally from Asia Minor. It was later adapted by Muslim artisans into a highly formalised form of intertwined flowers and plants.

The Qur'aan, the Muslim holy book, was revealed to the Prophet Muhammad (pbuh) by the Angel Gabriel. Its verses are often inscribed in beautiful patterns by calligraphers.

First published in 2005 by Mantra Lingua Ltd.
Global House, 303 Ballards Lane, London N12 8NP
www.mantralingua.com

A CIP record for this book is available from the British Library